Mariju

Guide

MW00425132

BRADLEY VALLERIUS, JD

ISBN: 9781980885559

CONTENTS

VALLERIUS

INTRODUCTION

Last year the US marijuana industry employed 121,000 people, and in the next three years the number is predicted to soar above 291,500. It seems inevitable that more states and countries will legalize— first medical use, then often recreational use too. So imagine how massive the job market will be in 25 years when legal marijuana is the new global norm.

If you have ever wondered what types of jobs are created when a state legalizes marijuana, this book is for you. It is written especially for job hunters trying to gain an advantage, and therefore it has three important goals. First, to give you a general overview of companies in the marijuana industry and the types of jobs they create. Second, to improve your chances of landing a job by sharing insider wisdom and proven strategies. And third, to keep your expectations in check about what working in the industry is like.

Working in marijuana can be invigorating, but it happens to be one of the riskiest, most volatile industries there is. Most companies are in start-up mode, struggling with the usual chaos and deadlines that a competitive new business entails. But even as start-ups go, marijuana companies are especially complicated. They are frequently pressured to move swiftly— sometimes too swiftly— in building the right combination of people who cooperate well as a team. Not everyone proves to be a good fit. Turnover of staff is high because the business is so different and challenging. Plus, of course, there is always the ever present threat that the federal government could swoop in at anytime.

So yes, careers in marijuana are definitely more exciting than most other industries, and tons more new jobs will be created in the next three years. But there are also more hazards lurking in this industry than in others. This book therefore sprinkles healthy doses of honesty and skepticism on its broad industry overview, because in order to make good career decisions you must understand the industry's negative traits as well as its positive ones.

Book Layout
This book begins with the fundamental concept that every state is different. Basically it means you must tailor a different strategy for each state, a theme that underlies everything else you will read here. You can feel free to jump ahead if you are in a hurry to learn about a specific subject right away. But if you want to gain the most from this book, be sure to come back and read the earlier chapters. Each chapter is a unique and important vantage point for analyzing the complexities of legal marijuana industries and the issues that matter to job hunters.

Chapter 1: Different States Create Different Job Opportunities. Companies in several states are hiring employees in large numbers already, but in others they are stalling. Usually where markets are stalling, it is because the law is too restrictive to stimulate real job creation. And where markets are thriving, there is a good balance of licensed companies relative to the size of the customer base. This chapter explains the ways that job creation is dependent upon the law each state enacts. If the law permits only a small number of people to buy products, then companies cannot hire many people to make products. Thinking about states in terms of how much opportunity is created is immensely helpful to job hunters because you can spend more time focusing on states where opportunities are bountiful and less time in states where they are few.

Chapter 2: Common Industry Standards and Practices. Lab tests, seed-to-sale tracking, and over-the-top security are features in all legal marijuana states because they are necessary to ensure public health and safety. Lab testing ensures products have not been contaminated by mold, fungus, bugs, pesticides, and other nasty impurities that can harm consumers. Lab testing also detects the amount of THC, CBD, and other cannabinoids in a product, helping customers make better decisions about what products to purchase. Security is important because most banks do not provide accounts to marijuana companies for fear the federal government could prosecute them for aiding and abetting illegal activity. This forces marijuana companies to become cash-laden businesses that are perceived as attractive targets for criminal attack. Finally, seed-to-sale tracking ensures that licensed businesses keep precise records of their inventory so that items cannot be stolen.

Chapter 3: Hazards and Caution. This chapter explains some of the reasons why marijuana is probably the most volatile industry there is today. It is important for job hunters to understand and accept these risks because they are definitely real, and they definitely cause disappointment for some people. But some of them can be avoided if you know what to look out for. One unavoidable pressure point is the contradicting postures of state and federal law, which threatens every licensed marijuana company and every person who works for one. Another industry hazard is an overcrowding of dreamers and exaggerators trying to launch businesses. Many companies will not succeed, but unfortunately they frequently mislead and string along unsuspecting job hunters with promises they never fulfill. This chapter helps you identify these types of companies so you know to be skeptical.

Chapter 4: Legalization Takes Years. News coverage runs wild and people get excited whenever voters pass a referendum or lawmakers enact a law, but these events are not ends in themselves but merely spark the beginning of a long, drawn out process. It will be many more months until jobs are created. This chapter explains the messy politics, careful business planning, and other events that need to occur before licensed companies are ready to hire employees. Usually it takes about two years from the time a law is enacted until the first growers, trimmers, extractors, budtenders, and other entry level employees are hired. Knowing this can help you form realistic expectations about when and where jobs are created. People often get overly excited about marijuana jobs too soon, only to become sour and skeptical when it seems to take forever for companies to begin hiring. But that will not happen to you if you read this book because you will understand that things unfold in due time.

Chapter 5: Cultivation Activities and Jobs. Marijuana growers need many employees— more than any other type of business in the industry. Dozens of human hands are needed not only to care for plants, but also to harvest, trim, and package buds. This chapter gives an overview of the activities that occur at licensed cultivation facilities and the jobs they create. Cultivation Employees work in highly controlled indoor settings, cutting clones, feeding nutrients, and fostering plants to grow big, healthy, potent buds. Harvest employees trim plants, hang stems upside down to dry, and then snip buds into buckets for curing.

Chapter 6: Processing Activities and Jobs. Extracting cannabis oil and manufacturing infused products are the main types of activities that take place in a licensed processing facility. Together, concentrated oils and infused products make up as much or more in sales than dried buds, which makes jobs that entail researching, developing, and producing innovative new products one of the hottest tickets in the industry. This chapter discusses the main types of extraction techniques, including the use of carbon dioxide and butane as a chemical solvent. The chapter also covers the manufacture of infused edibles and topical skin products.

Chapter 7: Dispensary Activities and Jobs. A dispensary is the first and only point of contact for most patients and customers. It is therefore important that dispensaries are staffed with employees who are great ambassadors for the industry. This chapter discusses types of knowledge that a good dispensary budtender should possess and the skills used to help customers make well informed decisions. Selling to recreational customers is pretty straightforward, but selling for medical use usually entails extra layers of legal requirements for very different types of customers. Staff must provide legitimately informed information on subjects related to different marijuana products and their use for treating specific medical conditions.

Chapter 8: Ancillary Products and Services Companies. Licensed cultivation, processing, and dispensing companies employ the majority of people who work in the marijuana industry, but there are also many other businesses and professionals who support them, creating lots of good jobs in the process. This chapter introduces various types of service professionals who apply their craft to attract licensed marijuana companies as clients. Some specialize in serving only clients who are licensed marijuana companies, including law firms, marketing firms, and consulting firms. But there are also plenty of big national and international law firms, PR firm, and other consulting juggernauts who are eager to land a client in this space.

Chapter 9: How to Find and Apply to Jobs. The final chapter integrates all the information from previous chapters to develop a roadmap of proven strategies you can follow to improve your chances of submitting successful job applications. You will learn techniques to help you find reliable information and good job postings, attend events where you can meet the owners and managers of companies, and write effective cover letters that help you stand out from the crowd.

1 Different States Create Different Types of Job Opportunities

Every state and country makes its own laws legalizing or prohibiting marijuana. If you are a job hunter, the differences are important. In fact, one of the first things you should do is learn basic details about the law in whatever state or states—or even country— you want to work. Subtle differences between them affects what jobs become available and how employees perform them.

People tend to be somewhat familiar with what regulation looks like in Colorado and California, but it looks different in Midwest and East Coast states. In Colorado, for example, a licensed business could specialize in making just edible baked goods, such as cookies and brownies, and nothing else. In most other states though, a stand-alone kitchen cannot exist because the law requires a kitchen to be part of a larger facility that is licensed to perform processing activities. A state could even choose, like Hawaii, to allow no edible products at all.

The point is that when you understand a state's basic legal framework, you know what kind of jobs become available—and even when. Do not blindly assume every state will have an industry explode with tons of jobs right out of the gate. Some states are so restrictive that they will not create many jobs until the law loosens up. At least if you know that, you can keep your expectations in check when you are applying in a restrictive state. Someone looking in Texas, for example, should not get their hopes up too high in the near term because the state's law is so restrictive that hardly any activity takes place.

Different laws also affect how employees perform routine tasks from one state to another. Compare budtenders in Illinois and Colorado, for example. In Illinois, cultivation centers put every finished product into its own sealed container prior to shipping them to a dispensary. This means customers at dispensaries in Illinois cannot see or smell samples of bud quality before buying. They just have to trust that what is inside the bottle is good. In Colorado, however, cultivators can and do send large unpackaged batches of buds to dispensaries, and budtenders put impressive samples into display jars behind the counter for customers to see, smell, and compare. Many customers decide what products to buy based on appearance and smell. So budtenders spend a lot more time in Colorado compared to Illinois showing products to customers and explaining finer details of product quality. Plus dispensary workers in Colorado have to weigh, package, and label products, which does not happen at all in Illinois dispensaries.

Incidentally, customers in Illinois may not like it, but very good policy justifications support the state's decision to regulate packaging the way it does. When a product is packaged at the site of production rather than at retail, it is put into a sealed, tamper-proof container that receives a label containing several pieces of information confirming the identity and medicinal potency of the item. Sealing the containers makes is virtually impossible for anyone to contaminate them or skim any amount of quantity from them while they are in storage or transport. Also, the label contains a unique barcode ID which tracks the entire production history and any movements or transfers of a product. The barcode ID stays on the packaged product indefinitely, surviving through shipment to a dispensary and sale to an end customer. The Illinois model is therefore very tight in that is easy for regulators to inspect records to verify integrity and identify discrepancies. By contrast, Colorado's regulatory framework does not allow as much precision.

Legalization = Regulation Through Licensing

When a state legalizes marijuana, it creates a licensing system for businesses to produce and sell marijuana products. Often only a limited number of companies can obtain a license, and they must comply with strict government regulations and inspections.

Business licensing is common in many industries, not just marijuana, because it is an effective way to enforce rules that protect the public from the known risks of a particular type of business. Butchers, taverns, restaurants, banks, truck drivers, casinos, pharmaceutical manufacturers, and pharmacists all require some sort of license because their activities entail inherent risks that can endanger other people if they don't take proper precautions. So in order to obtain and keep a license, the truck driver must obey the rules of the road, which are designed to protect other people and property from injury. Likewise the butcher and restaurant must follow health code rules for safe food handling and storage, which are designed to protect other people from getting sick from contaminated food. And the pharmaceutical manufacturer must submit random samples of its drugs for chemical analysis testing to protect people from consuming substances which are not what they claim to be. Agencies of the state government have the power to inspect licensed businesses to ensure they comply with applicable regulations, and businesses who do not comply can have their license revoked.

Sometimes licensing serves a secondary purpose— controlling the market by limiting the number of companies who can engage in a regulated activity. This often occurs in so-called "vice" industries as a way to keep public consumption of a product or activity below unsafe levels. For example, not just anyone can open a casino whenever they want. A state typically awards only one or two or three casino licenses at a time. Besides keeping the amount of gambling under some degree of control, limiting the number of licenses helps ensure the success of the companies who hold a license. Imagine if three brand new casinos suddenly opened in your city— it will be harder for each casino to make enough money to survive than it would be if only one of them had opened. When there are too many, they might resort to crazy desperate measures in an attempt to undercut each other.

The same concept is true for marijuana companies. It is easier for five licensed cultivators to make enough money to survive in any market than it is for 25. If there are too many licensed producers, there is a risk that they will overproduce, causing prices to plummet to the detriment of all of them. Many states therefore limit the number licensed marijuana companies, at least initially, until the market stabilizes.

Types of Licenses: Cultivation, Processing, Dispensing

At the outset of legalization, lawmakers must carefully consider what kind of industry they want to create. If the licensing framework they decide upon is smart and performs well, then the industry will flourish, customers will be satisfied, and wealth and opportunities will be distributed fairly. But if the licensing framework is not smart and performs poorly, then the market will flounder, customers will be unhappy, and wealth and opportunities will be unbalanced.

We already discussed that one central question for lawmakers is how many licenses to create. A related question is what types of licenses should they create. Marijuana industries generally consist of three core functions from a regulatory perspective:

1. Cultivation activities: grow plants and harvest buds and other plant material;
2. Processing activities: extract cannabis oil from plant material and manufacture infused products; and
3. Dispensing activities: sell marijuana products to customers at retail.

Some states create only a single license, which conveys the right to perform all three types of activities. However, many other states license each of the three activities separately, which means some companies have the right to perform only one activity and others have the right to conduct only two.

Cultivation license: Cultivation businesses are the largest employers in the marijuana industry because they need lots of human hands to perform repetitive, labor intensive tasks. This includes not just growing plants but also harvesting, trimming, and packaging buds. Most licensed cultivators use compartmentalized indoor grow facilities that are equipped with sophisticated environmental control systems. All plants and products are recorded and tracked in inventory using seed-to-sale barcode tracking systems.

Processor license: Processing refers to activities that transform cannabis plant material into products that have a new and different form, including concentrated oils and infused products such as edibles, skin lotions, and cosmetics. Processors use various techniques to separate oil from plant material, thereby creating a substantially more potent product with less of the plant's undesirable ingredients, such as lipids and cell walls. Extracting cannabis oil generally entails the use of carbon dioxide or butane as a solvent to break up plant material at the molecular level. Large-scale extraction requires heavy duty machinery, equipment, and supplies. Manufacturing infused products entails combining cannabis oil with other ingredients following basic recipes in a kitchen setting.

Dispensary license: Dispensaries receive marijuana products from licensed cultivation and processing companies and sell them to customers at retail. Accurate inventory control and record keeping is important, especially in medical use markets where employees must verify that a patient is a cardholder and record their transactions to prevent them from buying more than the legally allowed maximum.

Ancillary products and services: Licensed producers and sellers of marijuana products create the vast majority of jobs in the industry, but there are also lots of jobs working for various businesses who do not "touch the plant," and therefore do not require a license issued by the state. Legalization creates business opportunities for companies who sell essential goods like grow lights, nutrient and soil materials, extraction machines, packaging containers, and lots of other tools, supplies, and equipment. There are also great opportunities for service professionals to specialize in solving the unique problems marijuana businesses face, including lawyers, accountants, architects, marketing professionals, and more.

Vertical Integration of Licenses

A vertically integrated business is one that has the ability to both manufacture its own products and sell them them to end consumers— no middleman required. In the marijuana industry, vertical integration means being licensed to produce your own products in a cultivation and/or processing facility plus being licensed to sell them at retail through your own dispensary.

Vertical integration has advantages in all industries but especially in marijuana, where sometimes all of the licensed companies start up from scratch at the same time and must compete against each other for years in an intrastate market.

Here's a simplified scenario to illustrate the point: Imagine two different cultivation companies, one is named Vivian's Vertical and the other is named Sally's Stand-alone. Both companies just finished curing a 5-pound batch of Blue Dream buds that are ready for sale. Because Vivian is vertically integrated, she can transfer some or all of the batch to her own dispensary where she will collect the retail price for every unit, we'll call it $200 per ounce. Sally, on the other hand, does not have her own dispensary as a distribution outlet. She must negotiate with one or more dispensary companies to sell the batch at a wholesale rate, rather than a retail rate. In some markets the wholesale rate is about half as much as the retail rate, so here we'll call it $100 per ounce.

Competing on these terms gives huge revenue advantages to Vivian's company over time. But it is more than just a revenue advantage. Budtenders at Vivian's dispensary have an incentive to recommend products produced in-house over other companies, which gives them an added performance boost. Plus, Vivian can price her products lower on the shelf, making them even likelier to be purchased while still realizing more revenue than Sally.

Now imagine how this imbalanced situation could play out over several years. Vivian's competitive handicap over Sally grows deeper every month because every month she makes so much more money, all other things being roughly equal. Vivian will pay off debts sooner and have better access to more financing to fuel research, hire top talent, develop better products, and generally expand her business. Meanwhile, Sally could be struggling to make enough money to cover her expenses under the strains of the competitive disadvantage. She is probably holding on to survival, hoping a change in law could one day make it easier for her to compete somehow. Otherwise her business is bound to become acquired by a more successful rival.

Different possibilities for vertical integration are possible in different states. In some states, every license is vertically integrated across all three types of core activities, which puts every licensed company on equal footing. In other states it is possible, but not mandatory, for a business to become vertically integrated. Naturally every company wants to become vertically integrated, but if only a limited number of licenses are available, then a company must be one of the highest scorers on every license application it submits. Only a few companies manage to pull it off in each state.

States generally follow one of these three licensing frameworks:

Model A: Each activity licensed separately: In some states, each activity is licensed separately. So if a company wants to do all three types of activities, then it must obtain all three types of license. It is also possible for a company to obtain only one or two licenses. Maryland and Ohio are examples of states which license all three activities separately.

Model B: Cultivator/processor license and dispensary license: Some states combine cultivation and processing activities under a single license, so any company who obtains the license has the right to perform both types of activities. Dispensaries are licensed separately. For example, Illinois' licensing framework consists of 21 cultivation centers who perform growing and processing in the same facility. The state's 60 dispensaries are licensed separately. Pennsylvania is similar, except it uses the term Grower/Processor instead of cultivation center for its production licenses.

Model C: All activities integrated under one license: In some states, every licensed business is vertically integrated under a single license covering all three core activities. So every company that is licensed to cultivate is also licensed to process and dispense. Cultivation and processing typically occur at the same facility but dispensaries must be located elsewhere. These states typically create only a small number of licensees. Examples include New York, Florida, and Hawaii.

Geographic Distribution of Licenses

So far we've seen that lawmakers are challenged to decide how many and what types of licenses to create. The next question is where should licenses be allocated?

States that follow the general trend of holding a competitive application process usually require licenses to be distributed somewhat fairly across a state to that economic stimuli can be delivered throughout the state's entire territory. These states typically divide their map into licensing districts of roughly equivalent size. Licenses for cultivation and processing are almost always distributed evenly so that each region gets an equal number regardless of population. In the case of dispensaries, however, it is wise to allocate more of them in areas that are heavily populated than in areas that are sparsely populated. Dispensary licenses are usually distributed so that each licensing district gets at least one, and more densely populated regions often get more. So for example, if the northwest region of a state has a large metropolitan city but the southwest region is populated only very sparsely, then the northwest region should get more dispensary licenses than the southwest region, but both regions might get an equal number of cultivation and processing licenses.

Illinois is a good example of the point. Enacted in 2013, the medical marijuana law created 21 cultivation center licenses and 60 dispensary licenses. A cultivation center combines the functions of cultivation and processing under one license. Illinois has 21 State Police Districts of roughly the same size spread over the entire geography of the state, so the law conveniently awards one cultivation center license in each district. Meanwhile dispensary licenses are distributed so that each State Police District gets at least one, and a handful of more heavily populated downstate districts get two. A total of 30 dispensary licenses are spread across the heavily populated City of Chicago, Cook County, and surrounding counties in the Chicago metropolitan area.

Permissive States Create More Jobs than Constrained States

Marijuana industries are booming in several states, but in others companies are struggling for survival. In states where companies are struggling, the biggest problem is legal rules that prevent customers from qualifying to register for a medical marijuana card. Usually this means the range of recognized medical conditions is too narrow. And often the requirements for physicians' certification of patients is too difficult and discouraging for health care providers. Simply put, if law makes it easy for people to buy products, then demand will be high and the industry can hire many employees. But if law makes it difficult to purchase products, then there will not be enough demand for employers to hire many people.

Job hunters can group states into a few basic classes:

Prohibition states: The most constrained states prohibit marijuana products in all forms. Here, no company or person can legally produce or sell marijuana for medical or recreational use. Hence no jobs are created at all.

CBD-only states: Some states have laws that do create

21

licenses for the production and sale of marijuana products, but the rules are so restrictive that relatively few people qualify to buy anything, and the choice of products is extremely limited. For example, in Texas intractable epilepsy is the only qualifying condition. Few jobs are created in these states because there is only a small number of companies.

You can probably regard CBD-only states as being in transition. Because legalization faces more difficult challenges in conservative states, proponents have been willing to make compromises so that at least some of the people who need it most can have access to medicines derived from cannabis. The law will inevitably expand, and when it does the companies who are already licensed will be first to scale up and create new jobs. Additional licenses may also be created, but it will take months for any new company to submit an application, obtain approval, and prepare its facilities.

Restrictive Medical Marijuana States: In the middle of the spectrum are true medical marijuana states that permit people with many different medical conditions to obtain access to many different products derived from marijuana. Patients with a medical marijuana card can purchase buds, extracts, and infused without limitations on THC amount. While these states do create a large number of jobs, they are restrained from realizing their true potential because the law is still relatively strict and cautious. These states are characterized by a narrow range of acceptable medical conditions and rules that are confusing or discouraging for certifying physicians. Illinois and New Jersey are classic examples.

Permissive Medical Marijuana States: Some medical marijuana states are more permissive than others. Instead of being confusing and discouraging to physicians and patients, these states have more flexible, open-ended rules, which results in quicker, easier enrollment of patients in the program. Maryland is a great example. These states create many good job opportunities.

Recreational Marijuana States. The most permissive regulatory models, obviously, are the recreational use states: Colorado, California, Washington, and Oregon. Business is booming in these states because there are few artificial constraints. Licensed cultivators, processors, and dispensaries hire new employees as needed. This is a great place to be a job hunter because plenty of companies are hiring new employees to help ramp up their business.

Legal Constraints on Customers

The most significant factor affecting the size of a state's market, and hence its ability to hire, is the number of consumers who can legally buy products. The success of a medical marijuana state is limited to the degree its rules make it difficult for people to register for the program. When it is easy for people to register for a medical marijuana card, you can expect that almost everyone who should get one will indeed get one. But if there are obstacles, then some people who probably should get a card will be delayed or prevented. Recreational markets obviously do not impose any undue restrictions on people's ability to purchase and therefore have fewer forces working to curtail job creation.

What medical conditions qualify a person for medical cannabis? Some states define their qualifying medical conditions in a very narrow, specific, and restrictive way.

What types of professionals can certify patients? In most

VALLERIUS

states only a licensed physician can certify patients to use medical cannabis. A state could, however, follow Hawaii's example and authorize nurse practitioners to do it. Few states authorize a dentist, chiropractor, acupuncturist, homeopath, or veterinarian though.

How helpful is the government's outreach and education program? In an ideal world, the state government would uniformly embrace new marijuana laws and provide a budget for its agencies to regulate and inspect licensed businesses effectively. Regulatory agencies would spend resources performing education and outreach programs that help facilitate the uptake of medical cannabis among people who qualify. Unfortunately a decent budget and strong public outreach effort is missing in some states. As a consequence, segments of the population remain uninformed or misinformed about the law.

Are government agencies adequately staffed? Some states clearly define the roles and duties of regulatory agencies and give them the funding they need to hire agents to do the job well. Other states hire inadequate personnel, provide little financial support and training, and are slow and painful for the public to deal with.

How difficult is the registration process for patients? In some states fingerprinting is required as a part of a criminal background check that can disqualify a patient from participating in the marijuana program. The fingerprinting itself is discouraging for some people, even if they have no disqualifying offenses. It comes with a fee too, of course, which also is discouraging for some people.

Legal Constraints on Products

24

Another way that laws constrain an industry's potential is by restricting certain types of products while keeping others prohibited. A state might prohibit the production and sale of edibles, for example. The effect of banning any product is to reduce the potential size of the market, and hence the number of jobs that will be created. In the case of edibles, it means the dispensary cannot upsell a brownie or cookie to the casual customer coming in to buy buds or dabs. It also means some people will simply forego the legal market and obtain what they want from other sources. For example, some customers who have minor children may be interested only in edible products.

Examples of product restrictions include:

THC Maximum Potency Limits: Some doctors and lawmakers worry about escalating levels of THC (tetrahydrocannabinol) in marijuana products. THC is the chemical in marijuana that causes psychoactive stimulation. Some medical states have enacted laws that prohibit products containing THC concentration above a specified threshold. Florida, Texas, and several other states have set the threshold extremely low because lawmakers are interested in legalizing only CBD while keeping THC prohibited. Alternatively, a state could just as easily place the THC limit at an extremely high level. For example, lawmakers in some jurisdictions have debated prohibiting buds with a potency higher than 30% THC, a point at which products cause significant psychoactive effects in most people. Very few buds even reach this level of potency, so such a rule would not devastate any market.

Edibles: Neither lawmakers nor the industry has figured out how to apply good rules for edibles yet. There is legitimate concern for child safety because products often look like delicious cookies and candies. Dosing mistakes are also common, and there are plenty of horror stories about trying edibles for the first time. Frequently a person eats a dose of the recommended size, then after an hour they don't feel anything so they decide to eat a second dose. Eventually it hits them, and sometimes they end up panicking in the emergency room. More often they end up sleeping for a really long time and complaining about a miserable experience. For these reasons and more, some states ban edibles, at least for now, until they figure out a good approach to controlling these problems.

Buds (also called flower): Some states want to discourage smoking, so they prohibit the sale of dried buds. You can only buy concentrates and infused products in these states.

2 COMMON INDUSTRY STANDARDS AND PRACTICES

The last chapter emphasized that different laws create major differences among the industries of legal marijuana states. In contrast, the present chapter focuses on the rules and concepts that tend to be similar in all legal states. Certain rules are essential in all industries as a means to protect customers and the general public from mistakes that could be committed by licensed cultivators, processors, and dispensaries. For example, any state that legalizes marijuana should have rules that prevent a company from mislabeling the potency of their products, whether intentionally or accidentally.

Security

State laws are paranoid about the physical security of licensed marijuana facilities. Many people, lawmakers included, assume marijuana facilities are attractive targets for criminal attack. The irony is that this true only because of inconveniences that are perpetuated by outdated federal laws. Most banks do not provide accounts or other services to marijuana businesses for fear they could be prosecuted for aiding and abetting illegal activity. So cultivators, processors, and dispensaries are forced to conduct many large transactions in cash, which means that at any time they could have large sums of cash in their facilities or transport vehicles. If not for outdated federal laws, transactions would not have to be conducted in cash, and marijuana would be no more attractive to criminals than diamonds, pharmaceuticals, and other legal goods. In other countries, concerns for security are less paranoid.

In order to reduce the risk of threats from outside criminals, laws impose heavy security requirements on licensed marijuana businesses. As a result, the security systems at cultivation, processing, and dispensary facilities can be quite a spectacle. Usually you notice features as soon you approach. A sign at the front gate or entrance door might alert you that the area is under video surveillance, and you may see one or more cameras pointed at you at all times.

If you like working in security, all of this should be excellent news. Legal marijuana industries create many security jobs, from providing a simple guard presence to driving transportation vehicles carrying products and cash.

You encounter most or all of the following security features at a licensed marijuana facility:

Security officer presence: Most states require a facility to keep a working security officer on the premises during all operating hours. Some companies use more than one during the busy daytime operating shift, and some even use at least one even on nights, weekends, and holidays when no other employees are present.

Video surveillance: Video surveillance is an effective tool for deterring employee theft. Most states require licensees to implement video surveillance systems that can operate around the clock and capture every inch of a facility's interior (bathroom and private areas excluded) and outside perimeter. In a big facility, this is an immense number of cameras and can render a severe burden on technology systems. Most states require licensees to save video footage for several weeks onsite plus several more weeks off-site. State inspectors usually have remote access to a facility's live security feed in case they should ever want to watch. And when conducting physical walk-through inspections, inspectors routinely check the surveillance system to ensure it is recording and storing footage properly.

Man-trap entrance area: Most new facilities are equipped with a man-trap at their entrance. The front door opens into a small enclosed area where a glass divider separates you from a security officer sitting in a control room. The front door locks behind you, essentially trapping you because the door ahead of you which leads to the rest of the facility is also locked. There is nowhere for a person to go until the security guard confirms their details as an employee or guest.

Log-in, log-out protocol: Employees and visitors must sign in and out whenever they enter and leave cultivation and processing facilities. Tracking employee movement is a vital part of deterring theft.

No cell phones or cameras: Even when not prohibited by law, most companies discourage employees from using cell phones and cameras in production areas, especially when they are supposed to be working. The security guard who greets you at the man-trap may insist that you leave your phone in your car or at her desk.

Visitor ID badges: Visitors must present a valid government-issued ID and record their basic personal information onto a visitor's log. They receive a badge that identifies them as a visitor and must wear it visible on their person at all times while in the facility. Often it is worn around the neck as a lanyard or clipped to a pocket or lapel.

Employee Agent ID cards: Employees must wear their own personal agent ID card with their name and photo visible on their person at all times. Often it is worn around the neck as a lanyard or clipped to pocket or lapel.

Restricted areas: Some facilities implement key card or biometric technology to authorize or prevent certain employees from entering restricted rooms or sections. A trimmer needs to be able to enter the trimming room and possibly the drying and curing areas, but she doesn't necessarily need to enter cultivation or packaging areas. Because they record employees' movements throughout a facility, key card access systems can be useful tools for proving accountability if there were ever an accident or mistake. Instead of keycards, a facility might use biometric scanning such as fingerprint, retina, face, or voice recognition.

Sending and receiving products and cash: Some states require two security personnel to attend a vehicle transporting a delivery of products from a cultivator or processor to a dispensary and back. The vehicle must be registered with the state regulatory agency and meet certain technical specifications. For example, regulations may require that products be put into a locked container which is part of the vehicle and cannot be removed from it. The vehicle might also be required to keep a private and secure direct channel of communication with its home base and the state police. Usually a shipping manifest listing all items being transported and specifying the date of delivery must be sent to the dispensary ahead of time. Some states allow vehicles on the road only during daylight hours.

"Seed-to-Sale" Inventory Tracking

Related to security is the fear that a company or its employees might be tempted to steal products or plant material. In a nightmare scenario, a company's managers could sneak excess quantities of product out the back door and sell them illegally across state lines. Another legitimate worry, though of lesser degree, is that trimmers, packagers, extractors, and budtenders could skim a few buds or dabs to enjoy at home.

Regulations are therefore equipped with rules designed to prevent plants, products, and materials from disappearing from records through theft or otherwise. The solution to the problem is rules requiring companies to use barcode scanning and computer technology to meticulously document all activities. The barcode systems are called "seed-to-sale" tracking because they record every activity from the very beginning of the production cycle (planting a seed) all the way to the very end (making a sale to a customer).

Seed-to-sale systems are used to easily locate and find detailed information about any plant, any batch of oil or plant material, and any finished product in a facility. All three types of facilities must use them— cultivation, processing, and dispensary— whether vertically integrated or not. All the licensed facilities in a state use systems that are compatible with one another so that data is transmitted seamlessly whenever items are shipped between them. For example, whenever a cultivator ships a batch of products to a dispensary, lab test results and product ID numbers remain tied to each barcode. Dispensary workers receive the products into inventory simply by scanning their barcodes. Even if laws did not require seed-to-sale tracking, most honest businesses would still choose to use it because it is such an invaluable tool for recording and analyzing data.

Record Keeping and Inspections

State governments regulate marijuana closely. Their power to make and enforce rules is broad and includes inspecting the physical premises of a licensed facility and all records that are relevant to the business. Just like the state Health Department conducts regular visits to the butcher shop and restaurant to inspect for compliance with health code regulations, a state agency with regulatory power over marijuana companies conducts regular visits to cultivation, processor, and dispensary facilities to inspect for compliance with marijuana laws. Inspections can be random or announced.

Inspectors observe and scrutinize the physical premises and all activities taking place there. They review records on paper and computer to ensure their legitimacy and integrity, especially the seed-to-sale inventory data. An inspector can request that any record, specific or random, be produced on demand. Regulatory violations have serious consequences, including expensive fines and potentially loss of license.

Typical records subject to regulatory inspection include:
- Employee training documents and certifications
- Crop input records and schedules
- Video surveillance archives
- Waste destruction and removal logs
- Weekly physical inventory counts of plants, plant material, and products plus seed-to-sale data
- Invoices and other transaction records
- Chain of custody forms
- Receipts and contracts for purchase of equipment, material, services, etc.
- Shipping manifests
- Independent laboratory chemical analysis reports
- Marketing communications

Product Safety

In consumer goods industries— especially where food, medicine, and cosmetics are concerned— a product should be made available to the public only if it can be done safely. In the case of marijuana there are three vitally important components to product safety, and a good legal system must make rules for all three. If these rules were absent, unscrupulous businesses would cheat the system and endanger the public by using pesticides, selling spoiled product, and lying about ingredients and potency.

Lab Testing: Like pharmaceutical manufacturers, marijuana cultivators and processors are required to submit their products to an independent laboratory for chemical analysis testing. When someone buys a bottle of Tylenol, they can see on the label that each pill contains 500 mg of acetaminophen. Good laws try to hold marijuana products to similar standards. When a person buys an eighth of an ounce of buds or a gram of concentrated product, they can see on the label the concentration of cannabinoid ingredients that the product contains.

There are two main objectives of lab testing marijuana products:
1. to detect the presence of contaminants.
2. to detect the concentration of cannabinoids.

Testing marijuana products is somewhat different than pharmaceutical products though. Whereas every pill from every batch of Tylenol is expected to have precisely the same dosage of ingredients every time, with marijuana some degree of variance is expected. The concentration of cannabinoid active ingredients can vary, sometimes widely, across batches grown and harvested at different times, even when the strain is the same. This is because cannabis plants are dynamic living creatures.

Product Labels: Marijuana companies are required to put lab test results on their product labels. This information is necessary to make sure people can clearly see the concentration of active ingredients in any product they intend to purchase and consume. Labels must also carry warning messages and legal disclaimers, which are necessary to make sure anyone who comes into possession of the product can clearly see that it contains marijuana and poses potential risks including temporary mental impairment. Warnings therefore advise to keep the product away from children and not to drive a vehicle or operate machinery after consuming.

Child-resistant packaging: Like pharmaceutical products, marijuana products must be put into containers that small children cannot open. The classic plastic bottle with push-turn cap is therefore a popular choice for many types of products, including buds. Another is the flexible pinch-and-zip pouch, which is ideal for edibles and syringes filled with cannabis oil. In states where products are packaged at the site of production, the container must be sealed and tamper-proof, which means that it is impossible for anyone to open the container to steal contents or contaminate the product without destroying the seal.

Employee ID Cards and Criminal Background Checks

Some states bar people from working for a licensed marijuana company if they have certain types of criminal offenses on their record. Frequently a state's excluded offenses include violent crime felonies and drug-related felonies— including offenses related to marijuana. A conviction in any state at any time is sufficient to bar a person. For example, a conviction in West Virginia thirty years ago can bar a person from working in Illinois today. Every state's law defines excluded offenses differently, so you many need to evaluate your own criminal record and then research what the law of your state says about it.

Some employers integrate the criminal background check into their hiring procedure. Upon successful completion of interviews, a prospective employee may be invited to submit fingerprints so that the background check can be performed. A state government agency or the state police usually receives the information and performs the background check in conjunction with the FBI. In other states, like Colorado, employers commonly seek to hire people who have already obtained a permit to work in the state's marijuana industry ahead of time.

People who pass the criminal background check receive an Agent ID card issued by the state government. Employees are required to wear their ID card visible on their person at all times while on the premises of the facility. The ID card is often clipped to the shirt or attached by a lanyard. If an employee loses their card, they must report it immediately. If a person is convicted of an excluded offense while employed at a licensed marijuana business, the state can revoke the person's agent ID card.

3 HAZARDS AND CAUTION

Most people find their jobs in marijuana deeply rewarding. In this line of work it is easy to feel good, believing you are making the world a better place, fostering progressive social norms, and making natural products that improve the happiness and healthiness of people locally. Eventually though, that honeymoon feeling you experience when you start a new job wears off, and you become alert to certain unique hazards of the marijuana industry. As with everything in life, choosing to work in marijuana involves trade-offs. You might gain passion and freedom that is missing in your current job, but you inherit new problems you will not find anywhere else.

Start-up Companies are Volatile, Especially in Cannabis

Start-up companies are inherently risky. They are newly formed teams of people who have not known or worked with each other before, and in this industry they face challenges they probably have not seen before. State laws and other external pressures force marijuana companies to rush to open their facilities quickly. And some companies are lead by owners and managers who have little experience building a new company or working in a closely regulated industry. Many of them do not know much about marijuana except that they want to make money from it. Some do not fully appreciate the difficult challenges that await them or they would not get involved in the first place.

Because of the fast and loose circumstances in which marijuana companies are formed, especially in new states, the personalities and backgrounds of a marijuana company's leaders probably have more interesting flavor and contrast than other places you have worked. Licensing competitions tend to attract people from atypical career settings. A person must have enough comfort in their career and financial portfolio to dare invest their money, time, and reputation in such a risky venture. Compiling a strong application requires a whole team of people with weeks of free time who can demonstrate that they possess immense knowledge about cannabis and related businesses, combined with a deep reserve of money.

Most owners come from traditional business backgrounds. Many start off knowing little about marijuana or its production and sale. Often it is just an opportunity for them to make more money in a new industry that seems certain to flourish. Since they lack knowledge and experience themselves, they have to partner with parties who do have actual hands-on experience, which usually comes from having worked in black and gray markets. Often their partnership is like a shotgun wedding because the parties are under a tight deadline to agree to terms and accomplish a hard task. Sometimes the parties later find it difficult to reconcile their different approaches to running a business.

If the partners are successful in obtaining a license— most are not— then they must follow through on all of the plans they described in their application to the state. In some cases they have to construct a brand new facility and acquire all the necessary fixtures, equipment, materials, etc. And then finally it becomes time to manage day-to-day operations. All of these things can be a challenge for any director or manager who is new to the industry. They will find themselves regularly spread thin trying to cover duties in multiple areas at once, and sometimes they may not have the right relevant experience to guide them. For all these collective stresses and other reasons, employee turnover is somewhat high in the marijuana industry.

Dreamers and Exaggerators

Job hunters frequently feel like they have been strung along or misled by a marijuana company. Part of the problem is that there is an over-abundance of companies trying to occupy the field, but unfortunately some of them just do not have what it takes to win a license. Honestly, a few of them probably could not manage any kind of successful business at all. Nonetheless, some people talk a pretty good game, and they often try to recruit people when there really is not any work to be done.

You must always be on the lookout for dreamers and exaggerators. If a company has not secured a license yet, beware of job offers. Their plans are merely speculative, and you cannot rely on them. Far more companies apply for a license than the number of licenses that are actually available, and nearly all of them believe they are going to win. They will tell you plenty of persuasive reasons why they are certain to win: they have the best grower, they have the most connected lobbyist, they know the sponsor of the bill, they have a friend at the regulatory agency, etc. Unfortunately relatively few of the companies who apply get to be winners. So always remember when dealing with a company prior to licensing that their plans may not work out. Also be sure to do some researching of the company, its founders, and their promises. Does the company seem professional? Do they provide specific details that can be verified? If something seems too good to be true, it probably is.

Even if a company you have been talking with does win a license, you still might end up feeling like they have led you on. They might cause you to expect that they will offer you a contract to commence work right away, but in reality most positions are not filled until the facility has been constructed, built out, furnished with equipment, and passed inspection. This usually takes several months at least, and it almost always takes longer than a company initially says it will. So you might be left hanging on for longer than they tell you, and you might wonder if they really have anything for you at all or simply enjoy giving you hope and then letting you down.

If the opportunity does finally materialize and the company makes you a job offer, do not be surprised to encounter a sloppy onboarding and contracting process, because most companies are brand new, inexperienced, and flying by the seat of their pants.

Contradicting Laws Create Uncertainty
No other industry faces challenges like the marijuana industry. It exists in a state of legal paradox. Although more than half of the 50 states help their citizens obtain medical derived from cannabis, the US government calls it an illegal

controlled substance. Navigating a marijuana company is therefore a stomach turning challenge.

Having to exist in this strange limbo of legal gray area is a real drag on productivity. It would be great if owners and managers could focus their limited attention and resources on technical strategies that will help their company succeed, but unfortunately significant amounts of time are wasted worrying about what US Attorney General Jeff Sessions will do. As long as marijuana is an illegal controlled substance federally, there will always be the specter that a devastating event could happen any time. The scariest threat is that a federal law enforcement agency could raid a business, shut it down, and prosecute the owners for crimes. But more than federal law is perilous. State and local governments also wield an uncomfortable amount of power over marijuana companies.

Marijuana companies could face legal problems at federal, state, and local levels:

Prosecution under US federal law: The US Controlled Substances Act classifies "marihuana" in all its forms as an illegal drug. During the Obama years, the US Department of Justice did not regard enforcement of this antiquated law to be a priority for allocating limited federal resources. This was a sensible policy because under US Constitutional law, it is the state governments rather than the federal government who hold power to make and enforce laws for the health and safety of people in their territory. Plus many states have for years been enacting intrastate regulatory models for medical and recreational marijuana with strict control over production and sale, during which time many social benefits have accrued compared against relatively few social harms.

Nevertheless, just because a prior president declined to enforce an outdated federal law doesn't mean a current or future president also will. While President Trump himself has had little to say about it, his Attorney General Jeff Sessions has expressed plenty of negative, uninformed ideas about marijuana over the years, including many during his tenure as Attorney General.

Revision or repeal of state law: Another potential threat to a marijuana business is the prospect that a state could modify its law in an undesirable way. A worst case scenario, though unlikely, is that legalization could be repealed. Repeal of a law is always possible whenever a vastly different legislature or executive takes over power in government— just look at how viciously the Affordable Care Act has been attacked by the current Republican President and Congress after becoming law under a Democratic regime. A complete repeal of legalization is not the likeliest way a state law will change though. What is more likely to occur is a change to state law which makes it more expensive for a company to operate or harder to compete. A simple increase in taxes or licensing fees would make operating more expensive. So would tightening regulations in some cases. The most undesirable change of all for a licensed business would be the creation of additional licenses that allow more businesses to start producing and selling marijuana products.

Change of local zoning ordinance: Local city and county governments can also present legal problems. A marijuana company must be a good and welcome neighbor or the local government can use its zoning power to force the company out. Local governments and residents frequently try to resist the location of a facility in their community during the application phase of legalization, though usually they are won over by the promise of local jobs and life changing medicines. But just because a facility gained approval initially doesn't mean it will always have the unconditional love of its community. If a company is a lousy neighbor or otherwise becomes disreputable, then the city council in some cases can revisit the zoning issue to change the classification of parcels of land so that the location of the marijuana facility is no longer permitted. And even if the company behaves like an exemplary and responsible neighbor, there is always the possibility that the next election could bring a new city council that has completely different ideas about marijuana.

Competition for Jobs

Competition for marijuana jobs is tougher than most people realize. Many people are excited about marijuana legalization, and just as many more are hungry for any type of work that will improve their current situation. When you apply for a position, you might be competing against 100 or more other applicants. It is easy for managers to find decent candidates. Therefore you need to stand out in the crowd or you might get overlooked, even if you are the best person for the job. The good news is you can follow strategies suggested in this book to improve your chances of submitting a successful application.

Many Jobs are Expendable

The majority of jobs at licensed cannabis companies are entry level positions. No special career or educational background is necessary to get hired for most of them because almost anybody can be trained to perform the basic duties. Meanwhile employers have a deep pile of job applicants who are eager to leap at any opportunity to replace a struggling worker. Unfortunately this means that many people who work in the industry are replaceable and most jobs are not highly compensated, including growers, trimmers, and budtenders. The good news though is that most of these entry level positions are quite enjoyable and insulated from the maddening stresses that owners and managers encounter.

Confronting Negative Attitudes About Marijuana

Cannabis will continue to be a divisive social issue for many more years. We all know people who insist that cannabis is sinful, criminal, dangerous, or whatever, and we simply never will convince them otherwise. Copernicus had a similar problem when he started telling people that the Earth is neither flat nor the center of the universe. So do not be surprised if grandma or grandpa is uncomfortable hearing about your exciting new career in marijuana. She has been told for 70 years that marijuana is bad, and that is what she tried to teach her children and grandchildren to believe. When someone takes something as granted for that long, it can be hard to convince them otherwise.

If you work in the marijuana industry, you naturally must defend your decision to work in it. You are always going to meet people who ask, "So what do you do?" You must try to be a good ambassador for the industry. Be graceful and respectful even to people who express negative and combative ideas. It is just one of those things that comes with the territory.

Generally, you will meet people all kinds of people with broadly differing attitudes about cannabis. Some investors are sneaky and shady about their plans to get involved in cannabis because they do not want anyone they respect to think less of them. Others are genuinely proud and excited at the opportunity to make good medicine and to work advancing progressive social policies, regardless what anybody else thinks. Some of the most intelligent and successful entrepreneurs in the industry smoke daily.

VALLERIUS

4 LEGALIZATION TAKES YEARS

This chapter is all about understanding how long it takes to create jobs after a law is enacted. You have to be patient with this industry. Too many people start spinning their wheels too soon, but they just cannot go anywhere if there are not any jobs yet.

Because of the careful and deliberate way laws and regulations unfold, there are optimum times to be searching and applying for jobs in any state. Although there is always a flurry of media attention in the days and weeks after a state approves a voter referendum or enacts a new law, these are merely the first steps in a long process. Legalization entails several stages that unfold over many months, and each stage involves difficult decisions for government and businesses. By the time the first licensed businesses are ready to begin hiring their first wave of entry-level employees, about two years will have passed since the law was enacted.

The purpose of this chapter is to enhance your job hunting strategy by showing that there is an optimal time to focus on any state. It often tends to be later than people expect.

Hopefully this chapter helps you adjust your expectations so that you can allocate your time and attention better.

Stages of Legalization

With the exception of the ballot initiative, almost every state goes through all of the stages described here. The amount of time spent in a stage can vary. These are meant to be loose approximations, not rigid absolutes.

Ballot initiative approved by voters: Legalization often begins with a ballot initiative approved by voters. Ballot initiatives are not the ordinary way law is supposed to be created. They are part of an exceptional procedure whose availability is intended to be confined to rare circumstances where lawmakers fail in their duty to enact good laws for the people they govern. Ballot initiatives generate lots of media attention, but they are merely the beginning of a long road. They do not specify or bring new legal rules into effect; they merely command the legislature to enact a law that will achieve the initiative's stated purpose. Recreational use laws almost always start with a ballot initiative, but medical use laws are usually enacted by the state legislature without having to be spurred by voters.

Law enacted by state legislature: The role of the legislature is to enact laws whose broad rules outline the basic structure of a state's marijuana industry and the responsibilities of various parties. Sometimes the legislature itself decides the number and location of licenses, other times the legislature delegates these decisions to one or more regulatory agencies. If the law is for medical use, it will define rules governing the physician-patient relationship, recognized medical conditions, and other issues in the health care context.

Under normal circumstances, lawmaking should be a slow, careful process with many parties participating in discussions about research and planning. But everyone knows today's legislatures are highly dysfunctional. Even when constituents clearly demand legalization, and even when legislators agree that they should enact a law, they still might fail if they cannot agree on the basic structure of the regulatory system.

Regulations adopted by government agency: When the legislature enacts a law, it delegates authority to a government agency to continue the work of making more finely tuned rules for the industry as necessary. Good regulations ensure necessary protections for consumers, employees, and the general public. It is wiser for a regulatory agency, rather than the legislature, to establish the fine technical rules for an industry because the agency is staffed with lawyers, scientists, and other professionals who have specialized expertise in a particular subject matter. Legislators, by comparison, are merely generalists who are too busy trying to pass laws and running for election to get bogged down with the trivial details of technical rulemaking. Laws therefore grants authority to whatever agencies of the state government are best suited to handle the responsibility. For example, in Illinois, the Department of Agriculture received authority to make and enforce rules for cultivation centers; the Department of Financial and Professional Regulation received authority to do the same for dispensaries; and the Department of Health received authority over physicians and patients.

By design, the procedure governing an agency's adoption of regulations is supposed to take months. It is important to do the job well the first time and not ram through rules that are flawed simply for the sake of making products available quickly. Perceived delays upset the public, but slowness is a better alternative than failing to protect consumer safety or creating unfair competition. Usually the agency must publish a first draft of proposed regulations anywhere between 30 to 365 days of the law's enactment. The publication of a first draft marks the beginning of a public review and commentary period that is imperative for ensuring that rules will be fair and effective. During this time, interested parties are invited to express comments and criticisms about the law. The agency must consider all commentary, and in some cases it might be persuaded to change one or more of its proposed rules. Following the close of the public commentary period, the agency gets another roughly 30 to 90 days to publish a final draft of regulations, using feedback from the public to make as many or as few adjustments as it pleases.

License Applications Submitted: Following publication of final regulations, it is time for the state regulatory agency to issue licenses for cultivation, processing, and dispensing. If a state is following the norm these days, then it has decided to license only a limited number of companies. There will many more applicants than the number of available licenses, so the agency must hold a contest to determine which companies should receive the precious few licenses. The goal of the competition is to identify which applicants are the best qualified. Applications typically require companies to submit hundreds of pages of information about their business plan, asking them to demonstrate the following in writing:

- Strength, character, and fitness of ownership and management team
- Strength of facility design
- Strength and sources of financial backing
- Strength of security plan
- Strength of business operating plan

- Strength of cultivation plan
- Strength of processing plan
- Strength of dispensary plan
- Strength of packaging and labeling plan
- Strength of written Standard Operating Procedures

Agency scores and ranks applications: In order to ensure that its licensing competition is fair, the agency must appoint an unbiased panel of people to read every application and score them on their merits. Naturally this takes a long time. Applications are filled with technical information spanning hundreds, sometimes thousands, of pages. Meanwhile the process is closely scrutinized by applicants and journalists, and any perceived mistakes or biases in selecting the winners could result in lawsuits that delay licenses from being awarded and upset the public. Therefore agencies must take the process slowly and carefully, which means it takes months to review and score applications. The more applications that are received, the longer it takes.

License winners prepare their facilities: Finally the agency announces the highest scoring applicants in each region. The owners and managers of winning companies can now commence real work. They are not ready to hire many employees yet though, because they still must complete several weeks of administrative and licensing tasks such as closing on real estate transactions and acquiring equipment and supplies. Some companies must build completely new facilities from the ground up, which takes months. Others will move into already existing buildings that require substantial modernizations and repairs. Before a facility can commence production or sale, it must be inspected by local authorities and the regulatory agency.

Licensed cultivators commence hiring: Cultivators are the first licensees to begin hiring employees because they are the front of the production chain. More than a year, maybe close to two years, will have passed since the time the legislature enacted a law and the moment a cultivation facility finally becomes operational. A handful of the licensed cultivators usually rush to be among the first to open. Then more and more gradually open over the next several months. Suddenly there are hundreds of new jobs.

Licensed dispensaries and processors commence hiring: Hiring at dispensaries and processors gets underway about two or three months after the first cultivators have begun hiring staff. There is no work for them to perform until a cultivator can supply them with plant material and products. Like cultivators, a handful of dispensaries and processors usually rush to be among the first to open. Then more and more gradually open over the next several months.

Industry stabilizes; law and adapts: Licensed producers and sellers are finally able to commence work, but there is bound to problems. No state should be expected to enact a flawless regulatory system on its first attempt. However, a good government should regularly review the fairness and effectiveness of its rules and revise them as needed. In some states this really does happen, but others get stuck with quirky, pointless rules for years.

5 Cultivation Activities and Jobs

Many human hands are necessary to grow cannabis on a massive commercial scale. Licensed cultivators therefore hire more workers than any other type of business in the industry. Employees perform tasks related to growing potent, healthy plants as well as harvesting, trimming, and packaging buds and other products. Cultivation facilities also provide jobs in security, inventory control, general management, and administrative support. A typical cultivation facility employs about 30 to 70 employees.

Indoor Facilities

In most states, cultivators are required to operate in enclosed buildings, and growing outdoors is forbidden. Several reasons justify this policy. An outside grower who is at the mercy of nature, the environment, and pests can produce only harvest in a year. In contrast, indoor growers can more easily protect against animals, bugs, microorganisms, and other threats that can harm plants' health and contaminate their buds. Also, indoor growers can produce harvests all year long by controlling plants' environment 24/7, ensuring that conditions are always within ideal ranges for optimum health and maximum size. Most licensees would probably choose to grow indoors even if it was not required by law.

The facilities of licensed cultivators vary greatly in size. Some are smaller than 10,000 sq. ft. while others surpass 75,000 sq. ft. Especially on the West Coast and in Colorado, many facilities have been converted from a warehouse or industrial building that once served some other purpose before being retrofitted to grow marijuana. Increasingly though, companies are building brand new facilities from the ground up, designing them to their own ideal specifications. Some companies choose to build greenhouse structures so that plants receive lots of natural light from the sun, substantially reducing the enormous electricity costs of artificial lighting. Overall, cultivation facilities are becoming increasingly more sophisticated in their design and efficiency. Competitive application processes ensure that only the highest caliber facilities are approved. Meanwhile architectural and workflow designs continue to improve as companies learn from experiences in other states.

The best designed facilities are compartmentalized into separate sections that are sealed off from each other so that different types of activities take place in each section. It is important to keep activities separated for many reasons, including environmental control, security, biosecurity, and worker and product safety. So, for example, post-harvest activities such as trimming, drying, and curing take place in separate sections from where cannabis plants are growing. Additionally, any section of the facility might contain several rooms. So returning to the post-harvest example again, trimming takes place in a separate room from drying and curing, which takes place in a separate room from packaging. In the cultivation section, plants in vegetative growth are kept in separate rooms from flowering plants. A typical facility also has sections devoted to a security office, general office space, packaging room, supplies inventory, product inventory vault, and front-of-house.

Environmental Control

In nature, cannabis behaves like a typical plant. A seed germinates and develops roots in the spring, then grows in size and leafiness for several weeks. When days start getting shorter at the end of summer, plants shift their energy to growing flower buds. Indoor cultivation facilities mimic and improve upon the conditions found in nature to produce large, healthy plants all year long.

A well designed facility has finely tunable environmental settings from room to room. Many use automated technology to keep rooms always within optimal conditions and are equipped with remote access control so that managers can view and adjust settings via a mobile phone app and receive alerts if any room should deviate from the normal range, even late at night when no one is present.

Environmental control settings include:

Lights: Plants in vegetative growth are kept in rooms where lights are on for twelve hours or more every day. Plants in flowering stage are kept in rooms where lights are on for eight hours every day. Lights emit rays in the spectrum range of 400 to 730 nanometers. Different managers prefer different types of bulbs and fixtures.

Temperature: Room temperature is controlled through air conditioners and furnace units. Cannabis plants generally prefer temperatures of 72-82°F when lights are on, and a slightly cooler 66-70°F when the lights are off.

Humidity: Humidity, the amount of moisture in the air, is important because it influences how much water plants drink from their roots, as opposed to using their leaves to absorb moisture from the air. When there is more humidity, plants pull more moisture through their leaves and therefore drink less from their roots. But when there is less humidity, plants drink more from their roots. High humidity is important in propagation because clones have not developed roots yet. Clones are therefore typically kept under domes which trap in moisture to create a high humidity environment that enables them to draw water out of the air. Beyond cloning, it is important to control rate of absorption through the roots because the roots are where growers deliver vital nutrients that plants need to consume.

Carbon Dioxide (CO2): Plant respiration requires carbon dioxide. Supplementing the air in a grow room with CO2 tends to produce plants that grow bigger and healthier. Cultivators pump enough CO2 into the air to reach levels of 900-1600 parts per million. CO2 detection meters should always be installed in rooms to ensure the range does not reach levels that are dangerous for humans.

Ventilation: With all the heat and moisture in the cultivation environment, air must be kept flowing evenly throughout a room to prevent accumulation of mold and mildew. Cultivation rooms are usually equipped with vents and ducts that introduce and circulate fresh air while expelling old air. Strategically placed fans also help control air flow in a room.

Biosecurity

An outbreak of bugs, bacteria, fungus or other foreign organisms in the grow area can be a difficult and costly problem to eliminate. An infestation can impair the health and size of plants and contaminate their buds. Any sign of infestation requires the immediate attention of managers and is bound to cause production delays, scheduling conflicts, and other inefficiencies throughout the facility. The longer an infestation endures, the greater the risk it could spread to infect additional plants. In a worst case scenario, an entire room of plants must be destroyed and the room thoroughly sanitized. Therefore it is important to take every precaution to prevent an infestation from ever occurring in the first place.

Biosecurity refers to practices and procedures intended to prevent pest, disease, and harmful biological agents. Most cultivators instill the importance of biosecurity to new employees as part of their orientation and training. Cleanliness and sanitation are cornerstones of good biosecurity practice. Employees must clean up their work areas, take out the trash, wash tools and put them back in their appropriate storage places. Most cultivation facilities keep a regular schedule for performing tasks such as sweeping floors, sanitizing tables, and scrubbing walls. Workers should wash hands before starting and returning to work. It's also important for employees to leave production areas and tell a supervisor if they feel ill or have a contagious disease or open wound.

Clothes and shoes should always be clean. Many cultivation facilities require employees to change into a fresh set of clothes when they arrive for work in order to prevent the introduction of tiny insects and pests that could cling to a person's street clothes. Loose, baggy clothing and items that dangle, like necklaces and hoodies, are discouraged because they can make unnecessary contact with plants and clean surfaces. Many cultivators provide hospital scrubs to their employees to wear while working in the facility. Employees may be required to keep a pair of close-toed shoes to wear only at the facility and never outside. Employees also typically wear hats, hair nets, and beard nets to prevent hair from falling into plants and products. Vinyl gloves are necessary when working with plants, buds, and products.

Seed-to-Sale Inventory Tracking

Laws require cultivators to keep precise records of plants, products, and even waste material. They achieve this goal by using seed-to-sale inventory tracking systems. Managed correctly, seed-to-sale systems enable a cultivator to physically locate and look up detailed information about any plant or batch of material in the facility. Many cultivators would choose to use these systems even if they were not required by law because they keep such excellent business metrics, which is vital to success in any venture.

Seed-to-sale hardware usually entails a computer console on wheels that is rolled throughout the grow area and into various rooms as necessary. The console is equipped with a barcode scanner attachment for reading tags and a keyboard for entering data. A printer for creating new barcodes is another necessary component, but it usually is not movable like the computer console.

A cultivation worker can retrieve information about a plant by scanning the barcode ID attached to it. Alternatively, if the employee knows the plant's ID number, she can simply type it into the computer interface to view information about the plant. She can find information about any plant, whether it exists now or was harvested years ago, including:

- The date it was created
- How it was created (seed, clone, import), and by whom
- Its genetic strain identity (Blue Dream, Bubba Diesel, Purple Haze, etc.)
- Identity of its mother plant
- Its individual plant ID number
- Its batch ID number
- Its present location in the facility
- Dates on which it was moved to a new location, and by whom
- Dates on which it received treatments- water, nutrients, pruning, transplant, and by whom
- Date of harvest, and by whom
- Weight of batch at harvest
- Weight of batch after trimming
- Weight of batch after drying
- Weight of batch after curing
- Dates of any removal of quantity from batch, and by whom

Every cultivator has its own standard operating procedures that employees must follow in order to avoid mistakes in inventory tracking. Employees are trained to get into the habit of doing activities the same way every time, such as keying inventory data in a designated sequence whenever a plant or batch of plants is moved to another row, table, or room. However, even when employees receive thorough operating procedures and good training, they are still prone to make silly careless mistakes entering data, which can result in plant counts, locations, and weights being wrong. This sometimes causes problems for an employee working downstream who notices data that does not make sense. This downstream employee must now report her finding to a manager, and someone must investigate when, where, and how the mistake was made. A mistake that persists a long time can branch out to touch many batches and sub-batches, causing flaws in multiple records.

Key moments in cultivation when data is recorded:
- A clone or seedling enters the system as part of a batch.
- A plant is moved to a different room.
- A batch of plants is moved to a different room.
- A plant or batch is chopped for harvest and weighed.
- A random sample is taken for independent lab testing.

Key moments in post-harvest when data is recorded:
- Trimmed plant stems are moved from the trimming area to the drying area and weighed.
- Buds are clipped away from stems into curing buckets and weighed.
- Finished buds are removed from curing buckets and weighed.
- Finished buds are packaged for sale or packed for shipment to a processor or dispensary.

Genetic Strains
In the eyes of many consumers, cultivators are defined by the genetic strains of cannabis plants they choose to grow. Some cultivators specialize in mind-bending THC-strains and spacey hybrids but grow few CBD-strains. Others do just the the opposite: grow lots of CBD strains but few THC strains and hybrids. These examples are two very different types of

companies who target two very different niches of the consumer market. Many cultivators are somewhere between these two extremes, growing a balanced variety of strain types. When choosing which genetic strains to grow, the most important question is "will it sell in this market?" But there are many other factors too.

Genetic strains can differ in the following ways:
- Anticipated weight at harvest compared to other strains
- Number of days required to mature to harvest
- General ease or difficulty of growing
- Natural resistance to pests
- Shape and density of buds
- Color of buds
- Flavor of buds
- Smell of buds
- Ratio, types, and concentration of cannabinoids
- Quality and concentration of terpenes
- Density and shape of trichomes

From a purely health care perspective, the ratio, types, and concentrations of cannabinoids is a strain's single most important trait. Most cultivators in medical markets therefore grow a wide enough variety of strains with diverse cannabinoid profiles so that customers can select products that are best suited for their particular medical condition and personal temperament. Experienced recreational customers are interested in additional characteristics that distinguish the buds of one strain from another, including smell, texture, density, color, flavor and more.

Often the name of a strain is supposed to indicate its genetic lineage, but one should always be skeptical. Like a racehorse pedigree, a strain sometimes retains a piece of its parent's name. For example, Blue Cheese is supposed to be a cross of genetics from one parent strain, Blueberry, and parent strain, Cheese. In many cases though, names are not the reliable indicators of lineage they purport to be. The reality is you could buy Blue Cheese from two different cultivators and they might have very different aesthetic traits and cannabinoid concentrations. This should not be a surprise when you consider that most strains originated in illegal markets where good records were not kept and lab testing was not a requirement. The only way to reliably verify a plant's genetic lineage is to perform a genetics test.

Sometimes a cultivator creates a totally new name for a strain. This is how you get names like Obama Kush. The strain could be a new one created from in-house cross-breeding. Or else it could be a strain that until now was called something else but just is not selling well. Changing the name is merely a marketing ploy that is supposed to attract attention and stimulate sales.

Propagating New Plants

The creation of new plants is called propagation. When it happens in nature, propagation entails the pollination of a female plant by a male plant. A fertilized seed falls to the ground, germinates in the soil, develops roots, and then finally shoots up and out of the earth as a young plant. In a cultivation facility, however, these steps are skipped in favor of a faster, easier method called cloning, which takes advantage of the plant's ability to regenerate.

Cloning requires a healthy adult plant, called a mother. Usually mothers are kept in a perpetual vegetative stage of growth in a room where the grow lights are on for more than

12 hours every day to prevent the plant from flowering. To create a new clone, an employee cuts off a small end piece from one of the mother's branches and then inserts it into a special soil medium or plug. Kept under high humidity for several days, the clone will generate its own root system and become a distinct new plant. The new plant carries the same DNA as the mother it was cut from, hence the term "clone." The term "mother" is a misnomer though. It is technically not a mother but a genetic identical, more like a twin.

Employees are trained to recognize the best location to cut clones from a mother's branches. Dozens of cuttings are taken at a time because not all of them will develop strong roots and survive. Clones are cut only from mothers who are in good health because if a mother is weak or diseased then her clones may become weak or diseased. Also, cutting clones can weaken a mother's immune system, so it is best to wait a few weeks for a mother to recover before cutting more.

Two Growth Stages: Vegetative and Flowering

There are two general stages of plant growth. The main difference is the amount of light required in each.

Vegetative stage: The first stage of a cannabis plant's life cycle, spanning many weeks, is called vegetative growth. Vegetative growth occurs in nature during the long days of summer when the sun shines for more than 12 hours. During this time, the plant's roots system expands beneath the soil while above the soil the plant's stem grows taller and thicker as more leaves fill the branches. To mimic nature's conditions in the cultivation facility, vegetative rooms keep lights on for at least 12 hours every day. Some cultivators keep lights on for up to 18 hours.

Flowering stage: In nature, cannabis plants respond to the shortening of daylight hours at the end of summer by shifting their energy from growing in outward size to developing reproductive organs (flower buds). Cultivators mimic these conditions by moving plants from vegetative rooms into flowering rooms where lights are on for only 8 hours every day.

Harvesting

Fostering a crop to grow into large plants with fragrant, potent buds is a satisfying culmination for the employees who work exclusively as growers, but this is not nearly the end of the work at a cultivation facility. Several activities remain, and the quality of the finished product is affected by how carefully or carelessly these activities are performed. A cultivator could grow the finest batch of marijuana ever, but if employees do a careless job of trimming, drying, and curing, then the final quality can suffer in taste, appearance, and potency.

When plants are ready for harvest, their buds are large and covered with sugary-looking trichomes. Several days before harvest, employees stop feeding nutrients to plants and give only water, in order to flush out any remaining stores of nutrients that could affect the quality of finished buds. Ideally, plants should be chopped at peak resin production, which skilled growers can identify by the color of pistils and trichomes.

Harvesting usually entails chopping a plant at its base, then cutting it down into smaller stem pieces that can be handled more easily. Protecting the purity of buds is imperative. Employees must handle plants carefully, making sure buds do not drag along the ground or come into contact with surfaces, soil, or other contaminating debris. Throughout harvest and post-harvest, employees must ensure that plants remain segregated in correctly labeled batches and no mix ups occur.

Trimming

After they are chopped for harvest, plants are taken to a trimming room. Employees in the trimming room, called trimmers of course, pluck and cut away the many leaves that surround the cannabis buds on a stem. This is necessary because leaves contain relatively few trichomes and are undesirable for smoking. Removing leaves also improves airflow circulation around buds as they dry and cure. Plus, a good trim makes a finished product look pretty and attractive, like a great haircut.

Trimmers cut plants down into short stems about 1.5 feet long so that they are easier to handle. First large fan leaves are cut or plucked by hand from the stem and discarded as waste. Then the leaves clustered closer around the buds are trimmed down with specialized trimming scissors. Once a batch of plants is completely trimmed, it is weighed and recorded in the seed-to-sale system. The weight of the batch's waste material and trimmings are also measured and recorded. Trimmed off sugar leaves, squiggly little buds, and other scraps of plant material are often separated so they can be put to further use, potentially in-house making hash and kief or transferred to a processing facility to be used for extraction.

Trimming by hand is the norm in most facilities today, but there are an increasing number of automatic trimming machines being produced. For now, human hands tend to make a more attractive product, but they take much longer than a machine to the job.

Drying and Curing

Buds still contain a lot of moisture when a plant is chopped for harvest— too much for an easy, enjoyable smoking experience. Buds contain about 80 percent moisture at harvest, and cultivators need to reduce the amount to about 15%, first by drying them in open air and then by curing them in a closed container.

After a batch of plants has undergone trimming, the buds remain attached to their stems. They are transported to a drying room where they hang upside down to dry for several days. Temperature and humidity are kept under close control, and fans may be used to keep air circulating. If multiple batches are hanging in the drying room, employees must make sure they are clearly separated from one another. Correct barcode tags must be kept with each batch to ensure proper seed-to-sale record keeping and to prevent mix ups.

After several days, buds begin to feel dry to the touch, which means they are done drying. They still contain too much moisture deep in their centers, however. So the next step after drying is to sweat the moisture out from the center of the buds in a process called curing. To commence curing, employees snip the buds off their stems and commingle them into buckets or jars that are sealed air tight and left to sit. The buds sweat out moisture over time, becoming evenly moist on the inside and out. Employees must occasionally "burp" the bucket, by lifting the lid to release humidity and introduce fresh air, thereby preventing mold. Employees must also occasionally churn or rotate the bucket to promote even distribution of moisture across all of the buds. Buds are sufficiently cured when moisture levels hold steady at a pre-determined level (about 10-15%) for two days. A batch of buds is usually in a curing bucket for about 10 to 15 days.

Laboratory Testing

One of the great virtues of legal marijuana production over black market production is that regulations ensure to a reasonable degree that products are both:

1. free from contamination, and
2. as potent as their labels claim.

Good laws require a random sample from every batch of buds or derived product to be analyzed by an independent laboratory before it can be sold. In the case of buds, the optimum time for testing is at the end of curing because moisture has finally been expelled by this point, and the composition of cannabinoids has stabilized. A sample is usually composed of several randomly selected pieces of different buds from the same batch, which are then ground together. The sample should be fairly representative of the batch as a whole.

The integrity of lab test results is assured by the legal requirement that laboratories be completely independent from any licensed marijuana company, meaning that the owners and managers of a lab cannot also be owners or employees of a licensee and therefore have no incentive to lie about or manipulate results. Independent labs are subject to regulation and inspection by state regulatory agencies to ensure they use acceptable equipment and methods to perform tests.

Contaminants: One goal of lab testing is to detect whether any harmful contaminants are present in a sample. If any contaminants are detected, the batch from which it came cannot be sold.

Laws typically require lab testing to check for the following contaminants:
- Heavy metals
- Microbiological contaminants
- Mycotoxins (fungus)
- Pesticide active ingredients
- Residual solvents

Cannabinoid Active Ingredients: A second goal of lab testing is to determine the concentration of cannabinoids that are present in a sample. The results of lab tests are printed on product labels to help customers make better purchasing decisions.

Laws typically require labs to test for concentration percentages of these cannabinoids, at a minimum:
- Delta-9-tetrahydrocannabinol (THC)
- Tetrahydrocannabinolic acid (THCA)
- Cannabidiol (CBD)
- Cannabidiolic acid (CBDA)

Storing buds and plant material

Batches of buds that have finished curing are usually stored in a restricted access vault. All the buds from one batch are stored together in their own large container, such as a bucket or jar, in order to keep them segregated from other batches. A batch is a group of plants of the same genetic strain that were planted at the same time and harvested at the same time.

Every jar or bucket in the vault is labeled with important identifying information about the batch it contains, including the batch's barcode ID number, strain name, harvest date, and lab results. If a company keeps trimming scraps that it plans to sell or use for processing, it might store the material in the same vault as its batches of buds or in a separate one. The material must likewise be labeled with important identifying information and segregated by batch.

Accurate weighing and record keeping are critical in packaging and storage. Every batch is weighed before it enters the vault, and the weight is recorded into the seed-to-sale system. In order to reduce internal theft, only authorized employees may enter the vault, and any time an employee removes a quantity of buds from a batch she must enter it into the seed-to-sale system. This way if any product were to go missing, a discrepancy would appear in the records.

Whenever a dispensary places an order to purchase buds, an authorized employee enters the vault to weigh out the amount requested from the batch requested and records the amount removed into the seed-to-sale system, which automatically adjusts downward the quantity of buds remaining in the batch. For example, if a dispensary wants to buy nine ounces from a batch of Blue Dream harvested on 8/27 having batch ID #3273, then the authorized employee would enter the vault, locate the bucket containing Blue Dream batch #3273, weigh out nine ounces, and then access the seed-to-sale computer interface to record the removal. In order to prevent mix ups, employees should weigh one batch at a time, even if filling an order for multiple batches.

Packaging and Labeling

Some states require final packaging of products to take place at the site of production, which means cultivators must break down batches of buds into small units and put each one into its own child-proof container. So continuing the example above, suppose that the dispensary wants its nine-ounce purchase of Blue Dream buds packaged into units that weigh 3.5 grams each (⅛ of an ounce). The packaging employee filling the order must divide the 8 ounces she removed from the vault into 72 smaller units that weigh 3.5 grams each. Then she must put each unit into the designated container for a ⅛ ounce unit of buds. Each unit size has a differently sized container.

The next step is to fully and accurately label each unit, which entails using the seed-to-seed system's computer interface to print separate barcode stickers for each container. The system automatically assigns a unique product ID number to each container, which is affixed as a label. The container also gets one one or more other labels showing necessary pieces of legally required information, including strain name, batch number, harvest date, lab test results, and warnings. Some companies have streamlined the process so that an employee applies just one label showing all the necessary information. Other companies spread the required information across three or four labels which must each be affixed by hand.

Some cultivators sell pre-rolled joints, and the process for packaging them is similar. Every facility has its method of making its joints. Rather than laying the papers out flat and then rolling them between the fingers, which is cumbersome and time-consuming, employees are more like to use cone-shaped papers that are closed one end so that they just have to drop ground bud material into the papers, which is significantly faster. The last step is to place each joint into its own cone-shaped child-proof container and label it accordingly.

A large order containing many ounces of many strains can take several hours for employees to weigh, label, and seal. Therefore most cultivators employ a staff of workers devoted solely to packaging activities.

Shipping

After all the items requested in a dispensary's order have been finalized for shipment, an employee must create a shipping manifest identifying each item. This is necessary to ensure the order is accurately filled and that no product will disappear before possession is transferred to the dispensary.

Shipments to a dispensary can be large. If a dispensary has ordered multiple ounces of buds packaged into many small units of 0.25 oz. and 0.5 oz, then the shipment could contain hundreds of bottles, which takes up a lot of space. The shipping vehicle must therefore be a van or other vehicle with a large cargo area.

It is important to perform a final quality control check after finalizing an order for shipment and before sending the transportation vehicle off to the dispensary. At some cultivation facilities, security personnel are involved in the quality control check, which entails making sure that every package is labeled, that there is the correct number of products, and that the shipping manifest accurately corresponds to the shipment. When the vehicle arrives at the destination, an employee for the dispensary performs the same check to ensure the delivery matches what was requested and then scans each item with a seed-to-sale barcode reader to accept it into inventory.

Typical Cultivation Jobs

Different companies at different stages of growth have different ways of organizing and assigning duties to employees. On one hand, the first employees coming on board at a company that is a small new start-up might cover duties spanning across several areas of the facility. On the other hand, an employee joining a big facility that has already been operating for years in a mature market might be trained to specialize in only a narrow range of tasks. Some companies employ all of their growers and trimmers on a full time basis while others offer plenty of part-time shifts. Hourly wages, salaries, and benefits also vary broadly across different companies, and many of them use different names for positions which entail the same basic duties.

The most desirable qualities in cultivation employees are reliability and a great work ethic. Serious problems can occur if plants miss a treatment or other scheduled activity because employees failed to show up and take care of them. Employers simply cannot afford to keep workers who don't show up regularly and on time. The ability to get along with the rest of the team is also essential.

GROWER

A Grower is an entry level positions that works directly with plants. The position is sometimes called a cultivator or cultivation hand. Growers perform activities that are necessary to propagate new plants and raise them up to healthy maturity. The job typically entails spending several hours every day doing repetitive tasks, such as mixing and applying nutrients, pruning branches, cutting clones, combining soil media, transplanting, etc. A Grower might have to attend to thousands of plants on a daily basis. Some people are a great fit for the position and thoroughly enjoy the work, but some personalities find the duties boring and mundane.

Most companies do not require any special type of education, experience, or certification to become an entry level Grower. Of course prior experience growing plants is helpful, especially cannabis plant, but that alone does not guarantee an applicant will land the job. More than anything, employers are looking for workers who can be relied on to do their jobs as they are told without second guessing their manager because they think they know better. It is fairly easy to train new Growers, so the most desirable qualities in an applicant are reliability, a positive attitude, and the ability to work well with others. Knowledge and experience with cannabis are useless if the person is unreliable or does not get along well with others.

Typical Grower duties include:

Propagating new plants: Cut new clones from mother plant, then nourish and foster them for several days until a stable root system has developed. Cloning typically entails dipping the end of a cutting into a rooting hormone gel and then inserting it into a soil plug that is placed in a tray and covered with a plastic dome to create a high humidity environment.

Transplanting: When a batch of clones has developed a healthy root system, it is time to insert each of them into their own pot. Plants may also be transplanted a second time time, several weeks later while still in vegetative growth, when their roots have expanded to fill the original pot.

Vegetative Care: When plants are in vegetative stage of growth, employees give them water and nutrients according to an assigned schedule, while maintaining them under ideal environmental conditions and pruning as necessary.

Flowering Care: When plants are in flowering stage, employees give them scheduled feedings of water and nutrients, flush out nutrients during final weeks before harvest, and keep their buds free from contact with surfaces and debris.

Soil and Nutrients: Mix and otherwise prepare potted grow media, test and treat water, mix and deliver nutrients to plants.

Biosecurity: Follow company rules for clothing and hygiene, perform regular cleaning and sanitation of cultivation rooms and equipment, routinely monitor plants for signs of infestation.

Monitor environmental controls: Ensure that environmental control systems and equipment are functioning properly. Maintain ideal ranges for temperature, light, humidity, CO_2, and ventilation.

CULTIVATION MANAGER

Cultivation Managers are responsible for ensuring the cultivation team maintains constant, efficient production of big, healthy marijuana plants. Cultivation Managers instruct the team of growers how to perform their day-to-day duties.

Besides being knowledgeable and experienced at growing cannabis plants, a cultivation manager must possess many other skills that are essential to positions of authority and management. For example, the Cultivation Manager must be able to set schedules for the staff of growers as well as train them and instruct them on proper procedures for performing various tasks.

A Cultivation Manager usually must have specialized knowledge of botany or cannabis. She should also have experience managing other employees. Some companies prefer formal education and experience, such as a bachelor's or master's degree or doctorate in agriculture, horticulture, or plant science.

Typical Cultivation Manager duties include:

Leadership:
- Plan, make decisions, and instruct a team of Growers how to carry out activities in propagation, vegetative, and flowering stages of production.
- Train and supervise Growers and discipline them when necessary.
  Help develop and ensure compliance with standard operating procedures.
- Assist Human Resources department with employee performance reviews; make recommendations for hiring Growers.

Oversight:
- Perform or assign daily walk-through inspections of the cultivation area to ensure compliance with company policies and state regulations.
- Exert constant vigilance to detect and correct

various problems related to plant growth, health, and environment.

- Ensure efficient, problem-free cultivation of healthy plants in propagation, vegetative, and flowering areas.

Regulatory compliance:
- Ensure cultivation activities comply with state and local licensing and regulatory requirements, including occupational safety rules.
- Serve as point of contact for regulatory inspectors.

Record keeping:
- Maintain accurate and organized records as required by company policy and state regulations, including:
- Crop input and treatment application records
- Seed-to-sale inventory data
- Contracts for purchases of goods, materials, and equipment
- Human Resources, hiring, and training records
- Lab test results

Planning and scheduling:
- Work with the Post-Harvest Manager and Master Cultivator to coordinate and schedule the availability of cultivation and post-harvest areas and employees.
- Develop timelines for propagation and harvest of plant batches.
- Project supplies and labor needs on a daily, weekly and monthly basis.
- Manage seed-to-sale inventory system to precisely coordinate production with the needs of processing and dispensary departments or customers

TRIMMER

Licensed cultivators harvest plants all year round and therefore need a staff of trimmers to be available all year round. Trimmers spend almost all of their time every day removing leaves from harvested bud stems. A trimmer position is like a grower position in that it is an entry level position requiring no special background or experience, although compared to growers, trimmers have much fewer duties. Beyond trimming and maintaining the cleanliness of the trim room, there isn't much else for them to do.

Almost anyone can get a job as a Trimmer if they can demonstrate they are a good, reliable worker and a positive addition to the team. It also helps to have small nimble hands that are good at using scissors to make tiny precise cuts and can endure doing it all day. There is not a lot of responsibility. Usually you can daydream or chit chat without making mistakes, unlike other positions that require some attention to detail.

Companies differ in their hiring practices. A full team of trimmers could be scheduled on a regular full time basis. Or there could be many part time workers whose shifts vary each week depending on the volume of plants scheduled for harvest.

Typical trimmer duties include:
- Plucking and trimming leaves from harvested plants.
- Handling buds carefully to avoid damaging trichomes.
- Separating and weighing trimming scraps and waste material.
- Hang stems upside down in the drying room.
- Keeping the trim room immaculately clean.

HARVEST MANAGER

A Harvest Manager oversees the team of Trimmers. She coordinates the chopping of plants for harvest and all the activities that take place afterward, including trimming, drying, curing, and packaging. The harvest manager must communicate with the Cultivation Manager to ensure that space will be available in the drying and trimming areas and that workers will be on hand whenever batches are ready for harvest. A Harvest Manager also bears much responsibility for the final quality of products. Her employees must be able to remove plants from drying at the appropriate moment- neither too soon or too late. They must also know when to burp the curing containers. The accuracy of seed-to-sale tracking information is essential in a Harvest Manager's work. She may have to supervise and train employees to ensure that accurate barcode stickers continue to travel with a batch of plant material as it journeys through trimming, drying, curing, storage, and packaging.

Companies would prefer to hire people who already have experience working in or managing post-harvest activities, but such people are not easy to come by in some states. Knowledge of the sensitive timing element involved in drying and curing is an important trait that cannot easily be gained except through real experience.

A Harvest Manager's duties include:

Leadership:
- Plan, make decisions, and instruct a team of Trimmers and other post-harvest workers how to perform activities in trimming, drying, curing, packaging, and shipping.

- Supervise workers and discipline them when necessary.
- Help develop and ensure compliance with written standard operating procedures.
- Assist Human Resources department with employee performance reviews; make recommendations regarding hiring, discipline, and termination of Trimers and Post-Harvest staff.

Oversight and Planning:
- Chopping plant for harvest
- Trimming
- Drying
- Curing
- Packaging
- Labeling
- Communicate with Cultivation Manager to coordinate and schedule the availability of space for trimming and drying.
- Manage Trimmers' schedules to ensure enough labor is available to handle post-harvest activities on a daily and weekly basis.

MASTER GROWER

A Master Grower is a company's most knowledgeable person on the subject of cannabis, especially growing it. "Master Grower" is a generic term and different companies have different names for it, such as Cultivation Director. Sometimes the Master Grower is a company director or Chief Operating Officer. In some cases, the Master Grower is one the founders of a company and may have been responsible for designing or influencing physical aspects of a facility's design, including the floorplan, use of technology, and choices of equipment. She is therefore the person who ultimately commands all activities in a cultivation facility- all growing, harvesting, drying, curing, and packaging. She oversees both the Cultivation Manager and the Harvest Manager.

In order to hold this high level of authority, a Master Grower must possess a solid professional acumen to communicate with executives and owners of the company. Her duties could include splitting time between the corporate headquarters and the cultivation facilities. Because of her advanced expertise in marijuana compared to all the other executives and board members, she is a vital part of corporate level planning and decision-making.

A good Master Grower has several years of experience managing one or more legal marijuana cultivation facilities and understands the unique traits of a many genetic strains. These qualifications are difficult to come by in some states, particularly the Midwest and East Coast. Therefore Master Cultivators tend to enjoy great salaries.

Master Grower duties entail the highest level decision-making and planning, including:
- Directing and supervising all cultivation staff through oversight of
- Cultivation Manager and Harvest Manager.
- Choosing and budgeting crop inputs
- Scheduling crop cycles and required facility maintenance
- Developing standardized training protocols
- Maintaining a culture of professionalism
- Deciding what genetic strains of cannabis plants to grow

- Directing when and how much of a strain to propagate based on such factors as market demand, inventory supply, and ease of growing.
- Training employees, particularly managers
- Writing, reviewing, and revising Standard Operating Procedures.

PACKAGING SPECIALIST

Packaging specialists put bud products and plant material into containers for consumer packaging or shipment to a dispensary or processor. They usually work under the direction of the Harvest Manager. If the company is also licensed to perform oil extraction on the same premises, then packaging specialists also have duties related to edibles and infused products.

Packaging also entails labeling, and therefore the position requires constant attentiveness. Packaging activities are prone to absent-minded mistakes that can result in an incorrect quantity being delivered, or worse, mislabeling. Packaging specialists frequently access the inventory control system to enter weights and print barcode ID labels, sometimes several hundreds at a time. If processing occurs on the premises, packaging specialists also help weigh, divide, and package oils and infused products.

Some cultivators sell pre-rolled joints, and the process for packaging them is similar. Every facility has its method of making its joints. Rather than laying the papers out flat and then rolling them between the fingers, which is cumbersome and time-consuming, employees are more like to use cone-shaped papers that are closed one end so that they just have to drop ground bud material into the papers, which is significantly faster. The last step is to place each joint into its own cone-shaped child-proof container and label it accordingly.

Packaging specialist duties typically include:
- Creating or checking invoices and shipping manifests for accuracy
- Entering packaging data correctly into seed-to-sale system, printing correct barcodes and labels, and applying them to products without error.
- Collecting requested items from storage vaults whenever a dispensary places an order.
- Weighing and divide products
- Rolling joints
- Putting items into designated containers, applying labels to the containers, and sealing them

6 PROCESSING ACTIVITIES AND JOBS

Researching, developing and producing products derived from marijuana is an immensely exciting field with awesome possibilities for employees. Following nearly a century where it was criminal to possess marijuana for any purpose, companies now manufacture a wide array of concentrated and infused products on a massive commercial scale. Prohibition left a gap in human knowledge about cannabis compared to other plants, but legalization has already fostered a huge variety of highly tailored medicines and myriads of other interesting products. In mature markets, dispensaries sell as much or more concentrated and infused products as smokable buds. There is plenty of room for the field to keep expanding for years.

In many states, "processing" is a legal term that broadly refers to activities which transform plant material into concentrated or infused products. Concentrated products are created by separating cannabinoid active ingredients from the rest of the plant material. The resulting product is densely concentrated, sometimes reaching total cannabinoid concentration as high as 90%, whereas the most potent buds rarely reach 35%. Concentrated products are colloquially called dabs and marketed using terms that reflect their texture. Common names include wax, shatter, budder, and crumble. Dabs are consumed using a vape pen or dab rig, which function by applying enough heat that cannabinoids are released as inhalable vapor but not creating a flame so that none of the harmful byproducts of combustion are consumed. Sometimes cannabis oil is runny enough that it can be packaged into a plastic syringe (without a metal needle) and doses can be taken orally.

The term "infused product" refers to items made by combining cannabis oil with other ingredients. Common examples include edibles and skin lotions. Extracting concentrated oil from plant material is often the first step of producing an infused product. The next step is simply mixing the concentrated oil with the other ingredients of a recipe. Common edible products include brownies, cookies, gummies, chocolates, caramels, and mints. Infused products also include more traditional medicinal forms such as serums, sublingual sprays, capsules, and suppositories. Some companies even make vanity and cosmetic products, including massage lotion, shampoo, soap toothpaste, lip balm, etc.

Extraction is a Science (Not an Art)

Just as skill and care in the cultivation of plants and drying/curing of buds influences the quality of a final product, the same is true for manufacturing concentrated and infused products. Extraction is a science that demands constant attention and precision. Remember Walter White and Jesse Pinkman from the television show Breaking Bad— Jesse began loose and whimsical in his methods, believing himself an artist, and therefore he yielded product of a different quality every time he performed a run. Then Walter White taught him superior methods based on science, including strict precision, thorough preparation, and immaculate cleanliness. After that, Jesse produced superior product consistently.

A key tenet of the science of extraction is the age old expression: "Garbage-In-Garbage-Out." It means that if you use ratty, old, dried out trimmings of plant material, then you should expect to yield inferior oil. And conversely, if you start with higher quality material, you can produce more remarkable product.

CO2 Oil

Extracting with carbon dioxide is generally regarded as the gold standard method of producing cannabis oil. CO_2 extraction requires machinery and equipment that applies extreme temperature and pressure to force carbon dioxide through chambers filled with plant material. Under these circumstances, carbon dioxide diffuses deeply into plant material, separating essential oils from undesirable material.

Oil extracted using CO_2 tends to be soft and runny. It is typically amber brown in color. Because carbon dioxide leaves no chemical residue, the oil does not require additional treatment to eliminate hazardous chemicals. Nonetheless, sometimes additional treatments are applied to a batch in order to obtain an intended texture, such as wax, shatter, budder, or crumble. Oil that is runny and liquid may be sold in a plastic syringe container (without metal needle) or in a disposable cartridge that fits into a vape pen. If additional treatment is given to the batch, it could become a wax, shatter, budder, crumble, or other texture which can be consumed by dabbing or vaping and stored in silicone containers or sheets of wax paper. A skilled extraction employee using good plant material can create products with cannabinoid concentrations that reach up to 90% and beyond.

CO_2 is the preferred method of extraction for most licensed processors because it produces products with very high cannabinoid yields and great flavor, but especially because it is relatively safe. Carbon dioxide is safe to work with because it is non-toxic, non-flammable, naturally occurring, and has a low environmental impact. Products produced through CO_2 extraction are also regarded as safer for consumers since they never come into contact with a chemical like butane. Some people would argue that CO_2 oils are also tastier for never having touched butane and claim that more terpene aromas are preserved through this method. The biggest drawback of CO_2 extraction opposed to butane extraction is that equipment is considerably more expensive.

Butane Hash Oil

Another common method of extracting cannabis oil entails using butane or some other hydrocarbon gas as a chemical solvent in a similar fashion as described above for carbon dioxide. When used in specialized machines that control heat and pressure, hydrocarbon gas permeates plant material on a molecular level, separating desirable essential oils from undesirable plant components.

Extracting with butane frequently requires an additional action that is not necessary with CO_2 extraction called purging because hydrocarbons can leave an undesirable chemical residue in the oil. Lab testing regulations usually require checking for the presence of residual solvents, and products cannot be sold if they are detected above the legal threshold for safety.

Hash oil comes in a variety of textures, smells and colors, depending on such things as the quality of the plant material and precision of the machine and its operator. Like finished batches of treated CO_2 oils, the final product is frequently called wax, shatter, crumble and other names that reflect the product's physical texture and consistency. Hash oil is typically sold and stored in silicone containers or sheets of wax paper.

Equipment for butane extraction tends to be much less expensive than equipment for CO_2 extraction but more dangerous because hydrocarbons are noxious, flammable gasses. Licensed processors perform butane extractions using professionally installed closed loop systems which catch butane rather than allow it to escape into the environment where it could ignite and explode. Industrially designed ventilation and exhaust systems increase worker safety by decreasing risk of ignition and explosion. A lot of hobbyists perform butane extraction at home, but every once in a while they cause an explosion.

Hash and Kief

Humans have actually been processing cannabis for thousands of years using simple mechanical techniques. Hashish (more commonly called hash in America) is easily made using basic tools. Today's simplest methods use mesh metal screens as a sieve to break off and separate the crystalline trichome heads from the rest of the plant material. No chemical solvent is necessary used, just basic tools. A more efficient method of sifting, called bubble hash, entails putting plant material in micron filter bags and agitating them with ice in something like a laundry machine.

Trichomes look like a soft, salty, granular mixture when they are broken off and amassed into a heap. A heap of trichomes is called kief, which is sold as a product just by itself in some states. More commonly though, kief is pressed tightly together to form a densely compact brick of hash and is sold in this solid form.

Rosin Press

Rosin pressing is another solvent-less method of creating concentrated oil products. Rosin pressing has emerged only within the last several years. It is remarkably easy to perform, and fantastic oils can be produced using good plant material. The activity is a little like ironing clothes in that it entails using a heated machine to press down and flatten marijuana buds. The high heat and pressure forces the essential oils to ooze out of the plant material so that it can be easily collected. This is the same way olive oil is made. It is an extreme amount of heat and pressure, of course, far more than the household clothes iron can muster.

A high quality industrial rosin press is simple and safe to operate, and is programmed with automated settings that apply the ideal amount of heat and pressure over the ideal amount of time. There is little guesswork for the machine operator. Rosin pressing makes an oil which has a thick, sticky, solid consistency and is used for dabbing and vaping. Rosin press oil is pure in the sense that it contains to solvent residue, and neither winterization nor purging is required to remove undesirable substances.

The downside to rosin pressing is that it takes a lot of time and labor to create large homogenous batches, much longer than extracting with CO_2 or butane. For example, compare the process of making of 200 grams of rosin oil to the process of making 200 grams of CO_2 oil. When making CO_2 oil, the employee's most time-consuming duty is setting up the extraction machine and performing routine safety checks. Next she merely loads ground plant material into the machine's chamber and waits for the machine to do its work. Meanwhile she can attend to other duties. When the machine has finished, the resulting product is all one homogeneous 200 gram mass collected in a tray. By contrast, an employee can only make a few grams of rosin oil at a time. She has to perform the same procedure a dozen times or more to yield as much oil as one run of the CO_2 machine.

Before each pressing, an employee stuffs a mesh bag with marijuana buds, then simply presses a button to run the press for a couple minutes, then finally collects the small amount of oil the has been yielded. Then she must repeat the process again and add the amount yielded from the second run to the amount yielded from the first press. Then again a third and fourth and fifth time, etc until the mass of collected oil finally weighs 200 grams. If the employee is getting only 5 grams per press, she will have to repeat the process 40 times before having as much material as the CO_2 run.

Infused Products

An infused product is made by combining cannabis oil with other ingredients. Infusions are a broad and diverse class of products with many subclasses among them. The most common and obvious class is edible foods. More often that not these are sweet items like cookies, brownies, candies, and baked goods.

Another common class of infused products is topical medicines that are absorbed through the skin. These include balms, lotions, salves, serums, creams, and even massage oil. In the fact, the larger field of cosmetic products has been fertile ground for companies trying to develop and market healthy, natural lifestyle products containing CBD and THC. Almost any type of cosmetic product you can think of has been infused with cannabis, hemp, or CBD, including shampoo and conditioner, body soap, toothpaste, chapstick, moisturizing lotion, etc.

Many facilities where infused products are manufactured have rooms that resemble typical commercial kitchens with ovens, stove top ranges, sinks, coolers, and other typical fixtures. Infused products typically require the use of cannabis oil as a constituent ingredient. For example, the recipe for a chocolate bar might entail mixing many grams of CO_2 oil over low heat with cocoa, butter, and other ingredients.

Safety and Hygiene

The use of strong chemicals, extreme heat and pressure, flammable gases, and industrial machinery creates potential hazards in a processing facility. Processing employees must therefore follow written operating procedures designed to reduce the risk of accidents and mistakes that could injure employees or contaminate products and materials. Many operators have adapted operating procedures and safety precautions from other industries, particularly food and pharmaceuticals, because of natural similarities.

Standard operating procedures generally require employees to give regular maintenance and attention to extraction machines and equipment. To ensure a machine is working in satisfactory order, a checklist of items must usually be completed before commencing an extraction run. Then, following the extraction run, there is usually another checklist of items related to cleaning the machine, equipment, and tools and performing other routine maintenance actions.

Beyond keeping working areas in a clean, sanitary condition, employees must wear appropriate clothing and safety gear. The standard uniform is usually medical scrubs, close-toed shoes, and vinyl gloves. Goggles should be worn when high pressure machines are running. Occupational safety is such a vital concern that safety features are a major part of processing facilities' architectural design.

Safety features usually include:
- Gas detection and alarm systems for carbon monoxide and carbon dioxide
- Ventilation and exhaust systems
- Appropriate storage containers, shelves, and closets for carbon dioxide, hydrocarbon gases, and other dangerous materials
- Minimal explosive triggers and electrical risks
- Lab safety equipment such as eyewash and shower stations and fire extinguishers

Vertically Integrated vs. Stand-Alone Processors

A processor that is vertically integrated with a cultivation facility benefits from certain operational and recordkeeping efficiencies, whereas processors who are not vertically integrated endure disadvantages. Operational efficiencies and communications are fluid in integrated companies who perform cultivation and processing in the same facility. Here, the processing department enjoys first priority when it comes to selecting and reserving plant material it wants to use in its own extractions and not sell to competing processors.

By comparison, a processor bears hardships if it cannot grow its own plants but must rely on other companies to supply it with material. Here, the company must negotiate for the sale price of whatever material becomes available on the open market. The processor cannot simply take material free of charge from its own in-house cultivation department or rely on other suppliers to always keep it cheaply and adequately supplied.

Inventory Control

Processors are required by law to keep strictly accurate weights and records of their plant material and products in inventory. They do so using the same seed-to-sale barcode tracking systems as cultivators and dispensaries.

Depending on whether a processor is vertically integrated with a cultivation department on the same premises, inventory tracking can be markedly different in various facilities. On one hand, when cultivation and processing do occur at the same facility, authorized employees can essentially enter the storage area to obtain plant material for production runs whenever they need it. They must follow regular protocol to accurately weigh the material and record whatever they take into the seed-to-sale system. On the other hand, if the company does not cultivate its own plants, then all the plant material it uses must arrive via shipment from other companies.

When a shipment of plant material arrives from a cultivator, the employee who receives it inspects the items to verify they conform with what was requested as well as what is listed on the shipping manifest. If the shipment conforms, the employee scans the barcode of each batch of material to accept them into inventory and then moves them to the appropriate storage area.

From this point onward, every activity that occurs to a batch of material is entered into the seed-to-sale system. So if an employee removes 50 grams from a batch of plant material in order to use it in a production run, then the removal must be logged into the system. Then when the production run is complete, the employee must enter accurate weight and other details about the new form it has been converted into. So for example, an employee might record that this morning she removed 50 grams from a batch of Blue Dream plant material having barcode #0865 and 36 grams from a batch of Lemon Sour Diesel plant material having barcode #9623. Next she might physically combine the amounts she removed, thereby creating a new batch of plant material weighing 86 grams. The seed-to-sale system will generate a new random ID# for the new batch, we'll call it #6723, and will automatically reduce the weight of available Blue Dream and Lemon Sour Diesel in their respective batches accordingly. Next, when the employee is ready to perform an extraction run using the newly merged batch of material, she will record into the system that she removed the entire 86 grams from batch #6723 and used it in an extraction run, thereby converting it into a new product—concentrated oil. When she finally collects the oil after the run, she must weigh it and record the value into the seed-to-sale system, which will assign a new random barcode number for the new batch.

Lab Testing
The best regulatory models ensure consumer safety and protection by requiring a random sample from every batch of

concentrated and infused product to undergo chemical analysis testing by an independent laboratory. Products cannot be transferred to a dispensary for sale to customers until satisfactory lab results have been obtained.

The first main purpose of lab testing is to verify that products are free from contaminants. The danger with concentrated and infused products is different than the danger with buds. In the case of buds, there is a chance that mold, mildew, fungus, or bugs could be present in a sample. However, none of these dangers would be able to survive the extreme temperatures and pressure of an extraction run, so there is little chance they would be found in a chemical analysis test for a concentrated or infused product. Instead, the biggest concern about purity in concentrated and infused products is that a toxic residue from a solvent or chemical used to clean a machine could linger behind and taint oil products.

The second main purpose of lab testing is to determine the cannabinoid content of a product. Most laws require at a minimum testing for the cannabinoids CBD, CBDA, THC, and THCA, and some laboratories offer the ability to test for even more. Testing results must be printed on the labels of every packaged product, which helps customers make good decisions about which products to buy.

Processing Jobs

Processing companies vary greatly in their corporate structure and staff size. Some, but not all, are vertically integrated with cultivation activities taking place on the same premises. Many have existed for only a short while and are still just building their organization. Processing facilities generally need one or more managers with a chemistry science degree and several years of practical experience managing people in a relevant setting, such as a laboratory or production of food or pharmaceuticals. A team of extraction specialists is needed to support the managers, performing the more mundane tasks of prepping machines and material, running processes, and cleaning up afterward.

EXTRACTION SPECIALIST

An Extraction Specialist is a processor's entry level position that carries out the day-to-day duties of the extraction department. Different companies have different names for the position, such as Processing Technician and even extraction artist (though processing is a science not an art). A team of Extraction Specialists work under the direction of a Processing Manager. Depending on the size of the operation, the team could contain as few as two or three or as many as a dozen extraction specialists, employed either full-time or part-time.

Extraction Specialists prepare the extraction machinery and plant material for each production run following a rigid set of procedures in order to ensure actions are performed the same way every time. While the extraction machine runs over the course of a few hours, employees often time to perform their other basic duties, such as preparing and pre-packaging products or maintaining and sanitizing the work area.

A background in chemistry combined with knowledge about cannabis products is immensely valuable in an Extraction Specialist. However, even without a background in chemistry, a person can be a great addition to a team if she already has experience running extraction machines for another company. Different employers look for different traits in job candidates. Some might not care if an Extraction Specialists does not have formal chemistry education if there is a reliable manager on board who can supervise.

An Extraction Specialist's typical duties include:
- Grinding and otherwise preparing plant material for production runs
- Pre-packaging concentrated products into syringes, silicone, or plastic containers
- Performing weekly physical inventory counts
- Cleaning the work area, tools, utensils, and equipment
- Weighing plant material and trays of concentrated product
- Entering accurate information into the seed-to-sale inventory control system,

EXTRACTION MANAGER

The Extraction Manager is responsible for overseeing the team of extraction specialists to ensure the regular output of high quality concentrated and infused products. Many processing facilities employ only one Extraction Manager during start-up. If the company operates multiple facilities or in multiple states, then the Extraction Manager might work across all of the facilities, or the company may need to hire additional managers.

The Extraction Manager almost always has a chemistry or other science-based background. Often she also has experience performing management duties at some other similar type of business, like a lab or a production facility for food or pharmaceuticals. Advanced chemical science education and experience is necessary if the company intends to be innovative in developing new products. It is also immensely helpful if the manager has knowledge about safety rules in the manufacture of food and pharmaceuticals, including good manufacturing practices and certain Food and Drug Administration rules.

Typical duties of the Extraction Manager include:
- Planning and scheduling extraction runs
- Ordering plant material from cultivators
- Supervising the activities of Extraction Specialists
- Providing training
- Scheduling employee shifts
- Monitoring supplies and perform purchasing of utensils, equipment, packaging as needed
- Inspecting cannabis plant material
- Overseeing lab testing, inventory accuracy, and labeling

INFUSED PRODUCTS WORKER

A company might use various terms to refer to employees who work in the kitchen making infused products. Kitchen workers must be able to be around delicious smelling chocolates, caramels, and cannabis all day without being tempted to taste them. They prepare ingredients and equipment for each day's production and follow recipes to create batches of edibles, topicals, and cosmetics. The job also entails monotonous duties like spending several hours at a time putting cookies into plastic pre-packaging bags and sealing them, then putting them into final packaging pouches or bottles and labeling them.

It is imperative that kitchen staff be reliable, attentive, and stable under pressure. Some days feel rushed and crazy when many large batches are scheduled. No matter how tense the deadline feels, workers must keep their head in check to follow recipes correctly, avoid labeling mix ups, and ensure accurate weighing and counting.

A processing company might have a dozen or more different infused products that Infused Products Workers must routinely make. They usually make different items every day, depending on what is available in inventory and what has been ordered by dispensaries. Because edible products contain perishable ingredients, some items have a shelf life that can be as short as 30 days. Therefore such items are not produced until a dispensary orders them. Other items have a shelf-life as long as six months and can be prepared and packaged ahead of time, then moved to a storage vault until ordered.

Usually no specialized background or education in food preparation is necessary if a knowledgeable and reliable kitchen manager is on staff to train and supervise new employees. Food experience is definitely desirable though. Most people if given the choice would prefer to work in cultivation, trimming, packaging, or extraction rather than the kitchen. Therefore displaying particular passion and motivation for making infused products can take a prospective employee a long way.

Typical duties of Infused Products Workers include:
- Following recipes to make large batches of edibles, topicals, and cosmetics
- Mixing ingredients and pouring into molds
- Splitting up and weighing out units of product
- Performing decarboxylation of plant material
- Retrieving cannabis oils that will be used for

infusions

- Preparing the kitchen and equipment for daily productions
- Recording activities into the seed-to-sale inventory system
- Cleaning up afterward
- Putting finished items into pre-packaging wrap
- Adhering to safe food handling practices

INFUSED PRODUCTS MANAGER

An Infused Products Manager leads the team of infused products workers. The Manager coordinates production schedules to ensure inventory is always stocked and dispensaries are always supplied with products that are in demand. It is important that the manager already have significant experience working in food production following existing recipes and creating new ones. She should have thorough knowledge of safe food handling practices and be able to train and supervise employees.

Different kinds of products call for different cannabinoid ratios in the oil that is used. Consistently hitting the target range of cannabinoid concentrations is extremely important. Depending on the company's ability to obtain cannabis oil, this can sometimes be difficult because the ideal type of oil may not always be available. For example, a manager might usually prefer to use a blue dream oil having 45% THC and 13% CBD, but if the blue dream oil is out of stock, the manager must make due with whatever other oils are in inventory to blend something that will meet the desired cannabinoid range. An Infused Products Manager could have also have duties related to creating new edible and topical products.

- Monitor supplies inventory and purchase essential recipe items as necessary
- Keep accurate weights, measurements, and records of oils and finished products in use by the kitchen
- Perform math equations and balancing to follow existing recipes, create new ones, and produce products that hit desired cannabinoid ranges
- Schedule and direct Infused Products Workers

CONCENTRATED AND INFUSED PRODUCTS PACKAGER

A processing employees' packaging employees work to put cannabis oils and infused products in their designated pre-packaging and final containers. Packaging employees might help extract workers collect oil from trays, measure consumer size units (0.5 grams, 1.0 gram, and 2.0 grams, for example) and place them into their designated syringe, silicone, or wax paper. Packaging employees might also help in the kitchen, putting individuals brownies or cookies into shrink-wrapped plastic bags as pre-packaging, for example. Every pre-packaged unit of concentrated oil or infused product also gets packaged into its final child-proof container, labeled, and sealed. Packaging employees must be able to access the seed-to-sale system without making errors or mixing up products or labels.

Typical packaging duties include:
- Collecting items requested by a dispensary from out of inventory, packaging them, and preparing them for shipment
- Pre-package concentrated oils and infused products
- Use seed-to-sale inventory system to enter weights and print barcode labels

7 DISPENSARY ACTIVITIES AND JOBS

A marijuana dispensary is a unique type of business. Comparisons to other types of businesses are possible, but the differences are more significant than the similarities. In states that permit only medical use, a dispensary is similar to a pharmacy in that a person's access to pharmaceutical drugs is forbidden unless a physician recommends one. It is the same with medical marijuana— no access unless a physician recommends it. However, in a pharmacy the customer is limited to buying only the specific products that the doctor prescribes and in the specific amount she orders, whereas in a dispensary customers can select whatever and as many products as they want.

A dispensary is also a little like a tavern or bar, but here again the differences are more substantial than the similarities. Like a good bartender, a good budtender is sociable and charming, attuned to her customers and what they like. But unlike at a bar, dispensary customers in most states cannot lounge around and visit while consuming products on the premises all night long. A liquor store, with its broad assortment of wine, beer, and spirits has things in common with a recreational dispensary because customers are merely entering, purchasing, and leaving. But unlike a liquor store, the dispensary does not keep a regular and consistent supply of products from recognized brands like Budweiser, Seagrams, or Charles Shaw. Instead, products at the dispensary are small, limited batch offerings from local upstart producers.

Knowledge about Products is Essential

Knowledge about the varieties of marijuana products is the quintessential skill of a budtender. For many customers, the budtenders they meet are their only connection to the cannabis industry and therefore their only source of information about products. So budtenders have an important duty to build confidence in the industry by being cordial ambassadors and veritable experts on a broad variety of relevant subject. The array of product choices can be overwhelming, not just for new patients but also for regular users who are entering a legal dispensary for the first time. A budtender must have enough broad knowledge to help customers select products that will satisfy them.

While specialized knowledge about marijuana products is fundamental, it is not necessarily a prerequisite for getting hired. Dispensaries, especially in states that are only just starting up, frequently hire employees who do not yet know much about marijuana but have other great qualities and are motivated to learn. People can be trained to learn basic facts about marijuana products, but other essential skills like charm and personality are harder to learn if you do not already have them.

Good budtenders are knowledgeable or receive training in the following:

Genetic Strains. Many new customers do not realize there are so many different genetic strains of the cannabis plant having such broadly different properties that profoundly affect a user's experience. Budtenders must be able to compare and contrast bud products and demonstrate differences in appearance and smell where permitted. This should include explaining cannabinoid profile and other indicators of quality and potency. Customers also like to learn background information about a strain's reputation: what does the name mean and what are other people saying about how it makes them feel?

Cannabinoids. Cannabinoids are the chemical active ingredients in marijuana products that interact with receptors in the body to stimulate medicinal effects. Different cannabinoids have different effects, but most customers do not understand the significance of THC, THCA, CBD, CBDA and other vital information that appears on product labels. Therefore budtenders must help them. Some medical states require dispensaries to provide a PharmD, MD, or other licensed medical professional on staff to address questions and provide orientation for first time patients.

Product labels. A budtender must be able to explain the meaning of the legally required information that appears on a product label. Most states require labels to show cannabinoid concentrations, health and safety warnings, and ingredient lists, including allergens in the case of edibles, topicals, and cosmetics.

Edibles and Infused products. New customers interested in edibles should be warned not to consume too much too soon and to wait an hour before eating more if the initial dose does not feel like enough. A budtender should be able to explain what effects a customer might expect to feel after using a particular edible or other infused product. She should also be attentive to what ingredients are listed on product labels because some patients have allergies or other intolerances.

Reputation of cultivators and processors. The marijuana industry is more intimate and familiar than others. Licensed companies are not faceless corporations; they are local start-ups, owned and managed by people who live nearby and whom you may even know. Customers therefore tend to care more about the companies who make their marijuana products than they do other types of products. They have many questions about the licensed producers in their state, including what methods they use to cultivate and process, and they appreciate whatever information a budtender can provide.

Law and regulations. Customers need to be alert to the laws for safe use and possession of marijuana. In most states it is illegal to drive a car with an open product container, but many customers do not know this. Many also do not realize that even if recreational use is permitted, it still is not legal to smoke a joint on the steps of the courthouse or in other public places. Budtenders should therefore know the basic rules of legal use and possession in their state.

How to use accessories. Budtenders should be able to instruct patients in the use of various items the dispensary may carry. Many customers have never dabbed or vaped or smoked a pipe or joint before. Budtenders are sometimes asked, "How do I use this?" A budtender might have to explain how to grind buds, pack a bowl, roll a joint, or light up and inhale.

Budtenders Have Great People Skills

Besides being knowledgeable and passionate about cannabis, a dispensary worker should have great communication skills, a friendly attitude, and other positive personality traits. Providing great service and a personal connection is an important part of building great customer experiences, which can translate into increased sales and customer loyalty for the dispensary.

Many customers are learning about cannabis for the first time, and it can be overwhelming. The experience can be especially confusing or frightening for new medical patients. Some of them have recently received a worrisome medical diagnosis. They might have no idea how to take cannabis or how much, and they may fear it could make them feel weird, like they are "on drugs." Some have never smoked anything in their lives. The dispensary worker must make them comfortable and ease their fears. Good budtenders smile a lot, are good with conversation, know how to ask and answer questions, and seem to make friends easily. They recognize repeat customers and remember their taste preferences, always looking for new products or special discounts and promotions they might be able to up-sell.

To make orientation to the job easy for new budtenders, dispensary managers often provide training materials concerning standard procedure for communicating with customers. This might entail learning a short, loose scripted dialogue of questions designed to start conversation as well as generic responses to customers' frequently asked questions.

Confidential Customer Information

Privacy is immensely important for some customers, especially in medical use markets. Some customers want their medical condition and their use of cannabis to be kept secret from employers, friends, or family. A customer might reveal to a budtender that she was just diagnosed with a particular form of cancer because she wants help choosing the right products, but she doesn't necessarily want anyone else to know about it. The dispensary and its employees must respect her privacy.

The best practice for a medical dispensary entails upholding the same ethical standards as the healthcare industry, whether clearly required by law or not. In healthcare, professionals must maintain the confidentiality of communications between themselves and their patients. Applying the same rule to a dispensary means that employees must never talk to people outside the company about their customers. Job applicants who have training or experience in healthcare or social work are sometimes desirable job applicants because they understand issues related to privacy and ethics.

Style and Presentation

Every dispensary has its own unique presentation and style. You can see it reflected in the selection of furniture, fixtures, artwork, shelf space, lounge area, floor plan, and other aesthetic choices. Some dispensaries try to project themselves as serious and sterile for a strictly medical sort of feeling. Others can be chic and upscale, hipster trendy, or laid back casual.

A major part of a dispensary's style and presentation is the dress, attitude, and appearance of its employees. Employees convey as much impression on customers as aesthetic choices like furniture and artwork. So whenever you apply and interview at a dispensary, try to dress like you work there. If the dispensary is a serious and sterile place focused on medical use, then dress in a clean-cut, professional fashion. If it is a modern, laid-back place, then dress cool and comfortable, but nicely. Do whatever you can to learn about the dispensary ahead of time. You can look on the internet and social media to find pictures of how it looks on the inside and how employees dress.

Record keeping and Inventory Control

Dispensaries, like cultivators and processors, are required by law to use seed-to-sale inventory control systems that keep accurate records of all actions related to marijuana products. Since every licensed business in the state is required to use compatible systems, the relevant information contained in the product ID barcodes assigned by cultivators and processors translates seamlessly into dispensary systems.

When a shipment of products arrives, a dispensary employee must inspect every item to verify that they match what the dispensary requested as well as what appears on the shipping manifest. If this is the case, the employee affirms correctness and chain of custody by signing off on the shipment. Then she uses a barcode reader to scan each item into inventory and then moves them to a restricted access vault. Products remain in the vault until ready to be purchased by a customer.

Dispensing to a customer is the final part of "seed-to-sale." The product is scanned out of inventory when a customer buys it. In medical use markets every item a patient purchases is linked to their self in the statewide system in order to prevent anyone from purchasing more than the legal maximum. Also, if a recall of any product were to become necessary, then the dispensary and state regulator could quickly discover anyone who purchased recalled products to contact them directly. Recreational use markets more closely resemble traditional consumer goods sales where companies are not required to record individuals' identities and purchases. In case of a recall of recreational products, it would be necessary to put out a public service bulletin because there is no record showing who purchased recalled products.

Validating Customers

In medical use states, dispensary staff must ask patients to present their medical marijuana card before allowing them to enter the sales floor area to view and purchase products. The employee must look carefully to make sure the card is not a counterfeit and that the person pictured on the card is really the person presenting it. When a patient completes purchases at the register, the seed-to-sale system records their identity in order to prevent anyone from acquiring more than the maximum amount allowed by law.

In recreational use dispensaries, staff should be on the lookout for minors trying to gain entry with a counterfeit ID. Every ID card must be examined closely to ensure it is legitimate and that the person pictured on the ID is truly the person presenting it.

Vertically Integrated or Stand Alone

When a dispensary is vertically integrated with a cultivation or processing facility, it has easier ability to request and reserve bud strains and oil blends that are in high demand. Budtenders are likely to know more about products that are made in-house and might have bias for recommending them over similar products made by other companies. By comparison, a dispensary that is not vertically integrated must negotiate on the open market with licensed cultivators and processors to purchase whatever products it can get for its customers. Such a dispensary has significantly reduced ability to request and reserve popular products, and sometimes it might pay a premium to get them. On the upside, if the company is not vertically integrated, then its employees have no inherent bias toward any company so their recommendations can probably be regarded as objective.

Packaging and Labeling

In the new model of regulation favored in states like Illinois, Pennsylvania, Maryland, and Ohio, packaging of products does not take place at all in dispensaries. Products will have arrived from cultivators and dispensaries already packaged into their final child-proof containers. In these states, after a customer decides what items she wants to buy, a dispensary worker just needs to enter the products vault to retrieve the requested items and then scan their barcode to move them out of inventory and complete the sale.

Dispensaries in states that adhere to older models of regulation, such as Colorado, Oregon, and Washington, do perform packaging. These dispensaries must break down ounces of buds and trays of concentrated and infused products into individual consumer size units themselves. They might do so ahead of time or wait until a customer places an order for the item. It is important to accurately weigh and label every package and enter its removal into the seed-to-sale system. Especially at dispensaries that get a lot of traffic, packaging can be a burdensome task to which one or more employees must be devoted daily.

Dispensary jobs

The size of a dispensary's employment staff varies depending on various factors, especially customer traffic volume. In states that are only just starting up, traffic could be slow initially. The supply of products from cultivators and processors could also be small and sporadic at first. Therefore a dispensary may not need to hire more than a dozen people early on, but rest assured, it will grow in due time.

BUDTENDER

Budtenders work behind the counter, communicating with customers to sell products. Good budtenders are knowledgeable and passionate about expanding their knowledge of marijuana products. They also have friendly personalities and are great at communicating. A budtender should be able to answer questions about a broad variety subjects including product quality, how to use accessories, and the legal rules for safe use and possession. Above all, it is important for budtenders to build rapport with customers and create positive shopping experiences.

Budtenders perform several other general duties that are typical in retail settings, such as maintaining the cleanliness and appearance of the dispensary, stocking display cabinets, and closing the payment registers at the end of the business day. In medical use dispensaries, budtenders must respect customers' confidentiality and refrain from talking about them outside of work.

A budtender is a dispensary's entry level employee. Although knowledge about marijuana products is essential, already having practical experience is not necessarily a prerequisite to getting hired if a job applicant is motivated to learn and possesses other great qualities, especially in new states. Depending on the amount of customer traffic, a typical dispensary might employ a team of between five to twelve dispensary workers on a full time or part time basis.

Budtender duties typically entail:
- Help customers purchase products that will satisfy them
- Educate customers about subjects related to marijuana products as appropriate
- Retrieve products from the storage vault when ordered by customers
- Accurately records sales in the seed-to-sale tracking system and cash register
- Maintain professional dress and appearance
- Maintain cleanliness and professional appearance of the dispensary
- Perform routine physical counts of products in inventory

DISPENSARY MANAGER

The Dispensary Manager is responsible for nearly all planning and decisions at a dispensary. The Dispensary Manager takes direction from the company's owners and top managers, following their vision operating the retail business and instructing budtenders how to perform their jobs. In start-up companies that have not yet developed a cohesive public communications and messaging program, the Dispensary Manager could also have significant duties covering marketing and communications efforts. This could include planning public education and open-house events.

A Dispensary Manager must have specialized experience in

legal marijuana industries in order to keep the dispensary competitive with rivals. The Manager should be in tune with the latest products and innovations that drive customer demand. She must broker deals with cultivators and processors to keep the shelves consistently stocked with products and accessories customers want to buy.

The Dispensary Manager also performs the duties that are typical in most retail stores. This includes setting the schedules of budtender and other staff, providing and enforcing operating procedures, training employees, and maintaining a clean professional appearance in the store. The greatest responsibility of the Dispensary Manager is to make money of course.

Typical Dispensary Manager duties include:
- Recruiting, interviewing, hiring, and training staff
- Coordinate patient education programs and other events open to the public
- Review daily sales reports, reconcile discrepancies, and drive constant improvements
- Keep up with competitive intelligence in the industry
- Keep inventory supplied with top selling products, broker deals to order more products as necessary
- Maintain clean, professional appearance of the store
- Schedule employee shifts

8 ANCILLARY PRODUCT AND SERVICES COMPANIES

Previous chapters discussed the biggest types of employers in the marijuana industry—companies that are licensed to cultivate plants, process plant material, and dispense products to customers. These businesses cannot survive alone though. They need many other types of companies and service professionals for support. Like every legitimate industry, marijuana companies require a regular supply of essential goods and materials as well as specialized professional services from lawyers, accountants, architects, construction companies, security companies, branding and marketing companies, and more. A company might choose to hire some specialized service professionals to work fulltime in-house, such as lawyers, communications professionals, and security. Or the company could contract with a firm who specializes in the needed services.

Vendors of Goods: Machines, Equipment, Materials

Licensed marijuana businesses have a tremendous demand for physical supplies and materials, which creates opportunities for companies who are producers, distributors, and sellers of essential items. Companies need items that are unique to marijuana business, such as plant pots in cultivation and tanks of carbon dioxide in processing. They also need all the usual items that are essential in any place of business, such as paper supplies, light bulbs, computers, cleaning supplies, furniture, kitchen supplies, bathroom supplies, office supplies, etc.

Cultivation: Marijuana growers have the same basic needs as any other greenhouse, nursery, or indoor agricultural business. Basic material and equipment includes grow lights, fans, tables, tray, pots, scales, shovels, shears, gloves, potting, soil, nutrients, and a lot more.

Processing: Licensed processors need specialized machinery and equipment to perform extraction via CO_2, butane, or rosin press. Basic materials include tanks of butane or carbon dioxide, cleaning supplies, safety equipment, scales, glass and silicone trays, and various tools, utensils, jars, beakers, trays, and containers. If the facility produces infused products, then it needs basic kitchen supplies including stoves, ovens, coolers, baking sheets, pots, pans, spoons, spatulas, butter, milk, cocoa, sugar, etc.

Dispensary: Dispensaries need many of the same items as traditional retail shops: shelves, display counters, cash registers, lounge furniture, art decorations, and more. For the sale of marijuana products, they need display jars, packaging containers, and lots of relevant merchandise and accessories such as vape pens, dab rigs and equipment, glass bowls and pipes, grinders, storage containers, etc.

Independent Laboratories

Independent laboratories perform chemical analysis testing on marijuana products to ensure their purity and potency. A lab needs a staff of technicians to perform day-to-day testing activities and otherwise provide service and support to its cultivation and processing clients. Employees in the lab should have knowledge and experience in chemistry. A typical job could entail visiting production facilities to collect random samples, and performing various types of tests to determine the presence and potency of various chemicals or substances. A lab also needs business managers and people to help with administrative support, sales, and customer service.

Types of chemical analysis tests include:
- High Pressure Liquid Chromatography
- Gas Chromatography
- Thin Layer Chromatography
- Mass Spectrometers
- Real-Time Polymerase Chain Reaction

Communications and Marketing

Marijuana companies need good media and marketing strategies. They have to educate the public about marijuana products, a common goal shared by all companies, but they also have to distinguish their brand apart from the others. For someone who specializes in communications, working for a cannabis company could be a dream job. Few things could be more exciting than building a new marijuana brand and navigating it through a volatile and competitive airspace of ideas at the cross-section of politics, health, business, and culture.

In new medical states where it is priority for companies to raise the numbers of registered patients, companies must use communications strategies aimed at educating the public about marijuana products and the new law. In recreational use states, regular marijuana users have their own cool culture and lingo that communications need to connect with in order to build a strong brand identity. In many states the law restricts the advertising and marketing speech of marijuana companies, so communications professionals must always ensure they know the relevant rules in whatever state they are working. Also, sometimes sometimes publishers and media companies refuse to accept ads from marijuana businesses as a matter of policy.

There are boutique communications companies who specialize solely in marijuana. They claim to possess specialized background that enables them to provide highly tailored services to marijuana clients, including public relations, branding, advertising, social media, graphic design, and more. There are also huge international companies that already have a big multistate marijuana client or else are trying to get one. Meanwhile some companies prefer to hire their own in-house communications team for the sake of speed, economy, and control.

Legal Services

Marijuana companies face many threats to their existence spanning diverse areas of law. Some of their problems are typical in any type of business that produces and sells consumer goods, including contracts disputes, employee grievances, tax problems, real estate contracts, and regulatory compliance violations. But sometimes legal issues that would otherwise appear straightforward are complicated by the contradictory postures of state and federal law. For example, production facilities all over the country fret over OSHA regulations, but what role does OSHA play in a marijuana facility if federal law regards the business as violating the US Controlled Substances Act? And what are the tax consequences of realizing revenue from illegal activity? And what law applies to decide whether security guards can or should carry firearms in the facility or while transporting cash and products (i.e. illegal drugs under federal law)?

In states whose markets are longer established, such as Colorado, California, Washington, and Oregon, there are mid-sized law firms who specialize in serving marijuana clients exclusively. In newer states where there are fewer licenses, it is common for several big law firms to devote a young attorney to trying to build a new practice and attracting new clients whenever their state legalizes.

Licensing: Lawyers frequently participate in writing license applications for clients, racking up humongous fees in the process. Lawyers are a great addition to any team because no profession is better qualified to communicate with a government agency in persuasive and technical writing. However, most attorneys in new states do not possess deep knowledge about marijuana or its production and sale.

Litigation: Any business in any industry risks litigation sooner or later as a natural consequence of doing business. Accidents happen all the time and people back out or fail to comply with contracts all the time. But an increase in interesting new marijuana lawsuits is inevitable. For example, if an employee accidentally mislabels a product, the employer could find itself on the receiving end of a lawsuit if a customer consumes the product and then becomes overly impaired and commits a crime or accident.

Patents: Owning a patent on a killer marijuana product is an American dream. But as a species of living thing, cannabis presents questions about patentability, complicated by the complexity and diversity of cannabis genetics today. There are thousands of strains with broadly different genetic identities and outward traits. Is no strain patentable? Or perhaps is every strain distinctly patentable? How could a company prevent other people from violating a patent? In the case of derived products, companies are interested in obtaining patents covering specialized equipment, methods, or recipes for creating a product. Some would also like to find a way to efficiently isolate individual cannabinoids and mass produce them without having to grow plants.

Copyright: Hundreds of marijuana companies are emerging in isolated intrastate markets. Many have chosen tired, common concepts for their company name and logo. You can count on a percentage of licensed businesses in every state using a green cross for a logo and naming themselves with overused words like "Compassionate," "Wellness," "Nature," "Natural," "Remedy," "Health," "Clinic," etc. But if federal legalization is inevitable and interstate commerce is a natural consequence, then some of these companies will be a breakout success one day and want to protect their brand by preventing other companies from using the name and confusing customers.

General counsel: Marijuana companies frequently find themselves in precarious legal positions, sometimes without even realizing it until it is too late. They can benefit immensely from an in-house counsel who attends planning meetings and otherwise participates in oversight of the business. A lawyer who is adept in the relevant law and regulations can help keep discussions focused on compliant solutions while quickly dismissing ideas that can bear no fruit.

Contracts: One advantage of having an attorney readily available is the ability to quickly review, draft, and negotiate contracts. Marijuana companies engage in an intense amount of contracting during their licensing and start-up phases.

Security Services

Marijuana companies have an immense demand for security workers. Most facilities need someone to be present at the security desk during all operating hours, watching the security monitors and logging arrivals of visitors and shipments. Some facilities require a security guard to be present 24/7. Workers with security training are also needed to drive vehicles containing products and cash between licensed facilities. Some companies solve their need for security personnel by hiring their own in-house security team while others contract with an outside security company.

Government Inspector

Government agencies have important roles to play, and they need skilled employees to help them. Agents need to inspect premises and business records, which entails doing routine and random checks of the seed-to-sale system. In order to do a good job, the agency needs a whole team of inspectors who can go out into the field to routinely visit the premises of all the licensees.

Hemp

Hemp is something else altogether, regulated by a different set of legal rules than medical and recreational marijuana. "Hemp" generally refers to a type of cannabis plant that has little or no THC, the cannabinoid substance which causes psychoactive effects in humans. A license to produce or sell medical or recreational marijuana does not envision or entail the use of plants as fiber, fabric, fuel, or other industrial purpose. Likewise, states that enact hemp laws do not envision that plants grown by hemp farmers would be used for medical or recreational consumption.

9 How to Find and Apply to Jobs

If you have read the previous chapters, you are now equipped with broad, practical knowledge about the logistics of marijuana industries. You understand that every state enacts its own unique legal rules, thereby creating different types of companies and job opportunities. Yet despite their differences, every state shares important similarities that are necessary to protect public interests like security and consumer safety. It is important to remember that legalization follows a similar arc in most states, which entails several months of regulatory work followed by a competitive application process before any company gains the right to produce or sell marijuana products. But then suddenly a window of opportunity opens, and tons of new jobs become available all at once throughout the state. Equipped with this knowledge, you can now apply it to form smart job hunting strategies that will help you focus your time and effort on activities that are more likely to lead to success.

Step 1: Find the state regulator's website

Since every state is different, every state requires a somewhat different approach. So ask yourself, "What states would you like to live and work in?"

For each state, begin by exploring its law. Your primary goals are to discover how many licensed marijuana companies there are, where they are located, and who they are. You should also think about the state's legal rules that determine how many customers can buy products, which is relevant because job creation is dependent on the success of a market. Your chances of landing a good job are better in states where lots of people can buy lots of different kinds of products. Your chances are not as good in states where few people qualify and the range of legal products is narrow.

The best source for reliable information is the website of whatever government agency or agencies have power to regulate the industry. Different states delegate the power to different agencies. In some states it is the Department of Commerce. In others it is the Department of Public Health. If you do not know the name of the agency, you can find it through a simple Google search. Try searching for: "STATE cannabis law" or "STATE marijuana commission," replacing the word STATE with whatever state you are searching. The agency's website should be one of the top hits. You will recognize it as a government website because its URL contains a .gov domain extension.

Remember that job creation depends on the law's answers to these questions, which should be answered on the regulatory agency's website:

- How many licensed cultivators are in the state?

- How many licensed processors are in the state?
- How many licensed dispensaries are in the state?
- How easy is it for people to buy products?
- What types of products are legal and what types are illegal?

When there are many licensed companies, there are lots of different employers you can submit applications to. And when it is easy for people to buy a variety of products, then employers can keep expanding and hiring. But if it is a restrictive state with few licensed companies making a narrow range of products for a small number of people, then jobs may be few and far between.

Step 2: Research the licensed businesses in a state

Now that you know a state's legal rules and licensing structure, you can and should find information about the companies who are licensed to perform cultivation, processing, and dispensing. You should be able to find the name of every licensed company as well as the physical location of their facilities. You can usually find this information in the same place you find information about the state's law— the website of the regulatory agency.

As you learn about companies, you can start to build a hotlist of ones you might like to work for. Maybe you will discover that only a handful are located in cities where you would be willing to live and work.

You can use the following methods to search for more information about a company.

Google search: Use Google to search for the name of a company. If the company's name is a a common word or expression, like Grassroots, Compassionate Care, or Nature's Wellness, you might have to add the word "marijuana" or "cannabis" to your query in order to improve your search results. You may find that the company has already published a website with helpful resources, including job postings, personnel background, and a calendar of upcoming events. Even if the company does not have its own website yet, using a Google search, you might be able to find newspaper articles or other pages that contain useful details about a company and its founders.

Social Media: In an industry full of start-ups, many companies launch pages on Facebook and Snapchat several weeks or months before they are able to launch an actual website. In this case, the company is likely to use its social media channels to communicate with the public whenever it has details to share about upcoming hiring and events. If you want to be the first to know about announcements from a company on your hotlist, you should follow its social media pages.

Indeed.com: Many companies use Indeed for most of their recruiting needs. Search Indeed to see if any of the companies on your hotlist have created their own page for posting jobs. If they have, you can sign up to receive alerts any time they post a new one.

Google News Alerts: If you are really serious about following a company, you can sign up to receive an email alert anytime new information about the company is published online. Google will let you know you whenever a new article mentioning the company is published anywhere on the internet, whether it is news article, a blog post, a video, a podcast, or a page on the company's website. You could even set up an alert to receive statewide news if you are especially serious about keeping up to speed on business and legal developments taking place on a day-to-day basis. For example, you could set an alert for phrases like "New York cannabis" and "New York marijuana." A search like this can yield many hits every day though, and not all of them will be reliable or relevant for your purposes. For more information visit www.google.com/alerts.

CannabisPolicyAdviser.com: Managed by the author of this book, Cannabis Policy Adviser is dedicated to news and information about legal marijuana industries in the US and internationally. You can search for information about specific companies and find summaries of state laws and other relevant information. More info at www.CannabisPolicyAdviser.com.

LinkedIn.com: Like Indeed.com, LinkedIn is a convenient place for companies to share information about job postings. Plus, if a company has created a LinkdedIn page, you can view personal profiles of some of its managers and employees. This information can help you prepare for meeting and communicating with them at an upcoming event or interview. You might discover you share a personal connection or something else in common that you can talk about. You could also reach out directly to someone by sending a message, but exercise discretion, and have no expectations about how quickly you will get a response, if at all. Do not take it personally if you do not get the response you are hoping for, and do not let it dash your hopes. Some people do not check LinkedIn frequently, especially if they are very busy, and managers of marijuana companies are frequently overwhelmed with duties related to starting up the business.

Step 3: Networking

Standing out in the crowd and being remembered is important in the marijuana industry because jobs are highly sought after. You can usually assume that dozens of people are applying for any single job opening. One great way to be remembered is to meet the owners and managers of a company in person—then you are no longer just a name on a resume, but a real person with a face and personality. More than most other industries, marijuana provides lots of chances for job hunters to network with company leaders. If you keep your eyes and ears open, you will discover various opportunities to attend events where key decision makers of one or more companies are likely to be present.

City council and zoning board meetings- Marijuana companies frequently appear at public meetings of the local city council to advocate for their ability to locate a licensed cultivation, processing, or dispensary facility in the community. If you live locally and keep your ears open, you might find out about meetings ahead of time. Companies frequently present themselves to local government during the weeks and months leading up to a statewide license application deadline.

Most city councils are friendly and receptive to a new local business that will create jobs and stimulate economic activity. But sometimes the council is an uninformed or conservative bunch who is repulsed by the idea of legal marijuana. These are situations where a marijuana company needs and would appreciate your help. Sometimes companies need as much local support as they can muster at these public meetings to demonstrate that people in the community are in favor of legal marijuana and the jobs it will create. If the council invites comments from people in attendance, you could speak up for the company's efforts, and you can be sure they will remember you for it. Even if there is not an opportunity for the public to speak, you can still try to introduce yourself to the company after the meeting and let them know you are enthused about what they are trying to do. If the company does eventually get a license, you have an advantage over the other faceless applicants.

City council meetings do not always happen before licensing though. Sometimes it is not until license winners have been reported in newspapers that people become aware of plans to host a marijuana company. Local businesses frequently voice objections to the city council, which compels them to revisit the issue.

Fairs, Festivals, and Other Community Events: City and county fairs, festivals, parades, charities, and other popular local events are opportunities for marijuana companies to meet and win over individuals in the local community. Sometimes they put up a tent or booth to call attention to themselves and attract people to say hello. Hoping to meet good job candidates is one of their main objectives here. You might be able to fill out an application and meet managers who make hiring decisions. If you follow the strategies suggested in this book, you will sometimes learn in advance through Facebook, Snapchat, or a Google news alert when a company plans to be present at a local event.

Events hosted by a marijuana company: Especially in states that have only recently legalized medical use, companies frequently host events to welcome the local public, including open house mixers, grand opening ceremonies, cannabis education seminars, patient registration seminars, and even job fairs. As much as anything else, these events are part of a public relations effort intended to ease the community's acceptance of a marijuana business in the neighborhood and raise that company's stature and reputation. Come to these events prepared to make a great impression. If you go to a job fair, be sure to dress well and bring several copies of your resume and cover letter. Several individuals from the company will probably be present, and you can easily identify them because they will wear a shirt or hat with the company logo. Try to meet and charm everyone you can.

Marijuana Industry Conferences: Industry trade show and conference events are great opportunities to meet people from different companies and states. These events commonly span two or three days and feature exhibition space where companies set up information booths plus conference sessions where knowledgeable professionals discuss the industry's most pressing issues. Conferences and trade shows are great chances to network and learn, but they tend to be expensive. And most people who attend do not have recruiting on their mind but instead are focused on looking for new business deals and networking with other people who work in the industry. If you do go to an event, prepare a game plan ahead of time and stick to it. Do not get drunk. Keep your speech clean. Do not cuss or complain about anything. Dress well. Leave you resume and cover letter at home, but bring business cards if you have them. Talk to many people, even if you are introverted. Identify people and companies that you want to meet ahead of time, and do not get distracted from your goals.

Women Grow: According to the organization "Women Grow was created to connect, educate, inspire and empower the next generation of cannabis industry leaders by creating programs, community and events for aspiring and current business executives. Founded in 2014 in Denver, Women Grow is a for-profit entity that serves as a catalyst for women to influence and succeed in the cannabis industry as the end of marijuana prohibition occurs on a national scale." Women Grow has chapters in many metropolitan cities across the US, and each chapter meets about once a month. These are great places to meet both women and men who either work in the industry or are trying to get a start. There is price tag on admission, which is necessary to keep out riff raff. More information at www.WomenGrow.com.

Step 4: Finding and Applying to Jobs Online

For job hunters, a convenient feature of the marijuana industry for job hunters is that it is possible to know the name and location of every major marijuana employer in a state. With just a little effort, you can lean information about a company and create a hotlist of the ones you might want to work for. It is simple to keep track of the companies on your hotlist to know when they are hiring. You can even do it passively. Various methods are at your disposal:

Company websites: A company's website is often the best place to see its most recent job postings. Sometimes you can complete an application right on the website. Other times you might find an email address to which you are invited to send your resume and cover letter, even if there are no job postings yet. You should go ahead and do this, but do not set your expectations too high, and do not expect to get a reply. In all likelihood, your application is one of hundreds or thousands piling up in a generic company email box that no one will look at until the company is finally ready to hire. Usually by this time the pile of applications has grown so large and unorganized that it is hard to sort and manage. So you might want to submit another application a few weeks later because you cannot be certain the first one will ever be seen.

Sometimes a company's website allows you to fill out a generic job application form that asks questions about your education and professional history. These forms can feel overly cumbersome and take a long time to complete because they ask for information about every place you have ever worked or gone to school. Most people find these forms annoying. But when you fill them out correctly, they are excellent tools for hiring managers to easily search through applications to find what they are looking for. So it is important that you fill them out thoughtfully, honestly, and completely. Also, remember that hiring managers can and will search through their database of applications using keywords. For example, if someone needs to hire for a position in an edibles kitchen, she might search the database for people who have submitted resumes using words like "kitchen," "culinary," "food," "cook," "baking," "edibles," etc. This means that when you fill out a form, you should use words you want to be found for. For example, if you have experience trimming or want to work in trimming, be sure you use the word "trimmer" or "trimming" somewhere.

Indeed.com: This website is a tremendous resource for job hunters. Many companies post jobs directly onto Indeed, plus it aggregates results from sources all over the internet. You should visit Indeed regularly to explore new postings, and you can set email alerts to passively monitor for new opportunities and jump on them as soon as they hit.

If this is your first visit to Indeed, you may want to run a simple keyword search just to see the awesome power of Indeed and the sheer size of the marijuana industry already. When looking for jobs in the industry, be sure to search for both of the main keywords: "cannabis" and "marijuana." Searching for either of these terms will deliver different sets of results. Some companies use the word "marijuana" in their job postings but not "cannabis," while others do the exact opposite. Therefore you need to search for both terms to make sure nothing escapes your notice.

When searching broadly for "cannabis" and "marijuana," you will find a huge number of job postings, probably too many to easily navigate through, including many that are way too far away. Therefore you may want to narrow your results by confining your search to a particular city or state. For example, you could search for "Maryland marijuana," or "Pennsylvania cannabis," to find a smaller number of more narrowly tailored postings.

You can also use Indeed's alert function to receive a notice by email whenever a certain type of job is posted. You can set up just about any kind of alert you want. If you are looking for a job in Ohio, simply set up alerts for "cannabis Ohio" and "marijuana Ohio." You could also confine your search to a particular city or proximate distance from a location. You can set up alerts for the companies on your hotlist too. If the company has already created its own page on Indeed, you will find it through a simple search for its name. Then simply click "follow" to be alerted about new job postings.

Step 5: Cover Letters

Any time you have an opportunity to submit a cover letter, you should do it. Whether you are sending a resume or application via email or else uploading documents as part of an online application, a cover letter is the best place to demonstrate that you possess the important qualities a hiring manager is looking for. The cover letter is a great opportunity to explain the reasons why you are motivated to work in the marijuana industry. These details are essential in a competitive job market where it is important to stand out in the crowd. A plain resume and application by themselves are not enough because they do not allow you to explain memorable personal details about yourself. If you do not submit a cover letter, you must have stellar qualifications on your resume or else your application will probably end up in a pile with hundreds of other unmemorable applicants, never to be looked at again. But if you say good things in a cover letter, even you do not have stellar qualifications you might still score an interview.

A good cover letter explains positive and interesting details about yourself, which are intended to pique the employer's interest and make them remember you. Generally, you want to convey that you will be a loyal, motivated, drama-free, energetic, and reliable employee. Many people struggle with writing, complaining that it is a painful hassle they simply are not good at. But if this is your attitude, just relax. You do not need to write a marvelous piece of literature. Just write a short, friendly introduction from the heart, only a few paragraphs, and not more than one page. Just showing that you care enough to write a letter in the first place puts you miles ahead of people who do not.

If you struggle to think of what to say in a cover letter, try addressing these questions:

- Why do you want to work in the cannabis industry?
- Why do you want to work for this specific company?
- Do you have any special qualifications or knowledge related to marijuana, health care, social work, botany, retail sales, or other relevant fields?

VALLERIUS

ABOUT THE AUTHOR

Bradley Vallerius, JD is a lawyer who provides guidance about legalization to companies in the US and internationally. Vallerius provides business management and consulting in the planning, start-up, and stabilizing of licensed marijuana companies. His specialties include regulatory compliance, public relations, marketing, seed-to-sale inventory tracking, and human resources. Working as a recruiting manager for startup companies, Vallerius has interviewed and reviewed resumes and cover letters of thousands of job applicants for budtenders, growers, trimmers, extractors, security guards, and more. He knows firsthand the strategies that successful job hunters use to make a lasting and successful impression.

VALLERIUS

Made in the USA
Monee, IL
14 October 2021